EASTER ISLAND

Rapa Nui, a Land of Rocky Dreams

EASTER Island

Rapa Nui, a Land of Rocky Dreams

TEXT BY
José Miguel Ramírez
mataveriotai@entelchile.net

DESIGNED BY
Carolyn Fell G.
cfell@mail.com

PHOTOGRAPHS BY
Carlos Huber
hubercarlos@hotmail.com
Exceptions on page 188

DRAWINGS BY
Te Pou Huke

COORDINATION BY
Francisco Luco
fluco@nunatack.cl

I.S.B.N. :
956.288.638.7

PRINTED BY
Alvimpress Impresores
albertel@terra.cl

TRANSLATED BY
Berlitz GlobalNet Chile
Production3@berlitzglobalnet.cl

© 2000 Carlos Huber
First Edition 4,000 copies

All Rights Reserved. No part of this publication may be reproduced or transmitted in any form or by any means, electronic or mechanical, including photocopy, recording or any other information storage and retrieval system, without prior permission in writing from the publisher.

Contents

Prologue	7
Introduction. *A Unique Story*	8
The setting. *A Changing Scenery*	16
The origins. *Mystery Solved?*	22
The Origins Revisited	28
Organization of the ancient society	30
Crisis and adaptation. *The Huri-Moai Phase (1680-1867 A.D.)*	34
Orongo. Site of the Tangata Manu Competition	36
Mata Ngarau	41
The Motu. Manutara's Ancient Kingdom	42
Ana Kai Tangata. Cannibal's Cave?	50
Megalithic Culture. *The Ahu-Moai Phase (1000-1680 A.D.)*	53
The Ahu	53
West Coast	57
Tahai Ceremonial Complex	57
South Coast	62
Ahu Vinapu	62
Ahu Vaihu	63
Ahu Hanga Tetenga	63
The Moai	64
Rano Raraku	64
Carving, Transport and Installation	68
Ahu Tongariki	81
Poike Peninsula	90
Ana O Keke	91
North Coast	93
Ahu Te Pito Kura	93
Ovahe	94
Anakena	95
Ahu Nau Nau	96
Ahu Ature Huki	99
Inland Rapa Nui	102
Maunga Terevaka	103
Ahu Akivi	106
Ana Te Pahu	108
Archaeoastronomy	109
Ideology	112
Wood and rock carvings	115
Rongo rongo	120
Rock art	122
The ocean and fishing	127
The Underwater World of Rapa Nui	130
Tattooing, body painting and mutilation	134
The Living Culture. *Tapati Rapa Nui*	153
Final Words	186
Acknowledgements	188
Glossary	189
Bibliography	190

Prologue

If I climb to the highest point on **Rapa Nui**, the **Maunga Terevaka**, and look to the north, all I can see is the vast immensity of the ocean, but I know that the closest land is the Galapagos Islands, located 3,800 kilometers away. I turn slightly and look to the west. Again, all I can see is ocean. This time, 4,000 kilometers separate me from Tahiti and 2,000 kilometers from Pitcairn Island, the nearest land. I turn once more and face the south, where more than 5,000 kilometers of water lie between the Antarctic ice caps and me. Finally, I turn for the last time and face the east, and now, stretching before me are 3,700 kilometers of emptiness before reaching the coast of Chile in South America.

On this remote and lonely spot, lost in the enormity of the Pacific Ocean, was born one of the world's most fascinating cultures, one that is unique among its kind.

In a remote period of time, the island rose out of the sea, driven by the force of countless volcanoes.

At some point, the island became populated by a race of mariners who navigated enormous distances to reach her shores. They must have thought they were the only human beings alive on the planet because **Hiva**, their motherland, had sunk into the sea.

For many centuries, the island was fortunate to remain hidden on the horizon due to her isolation. Its inhabitants learned to live alone. There, segregated from the outside world, they forged one of the most extraordinary and solitary cultures on earth, a culture all their own. How it was able to evolve under those conditions and reach such a level of development is one of the island's true mysteries.

The colossal stone statues, the **moai**, are the island's most widely-known trademarks. Yet they are just one of many symbols.

This monumental "open-air museum" was unveiled to the European world for the first time more than three centuries ago, and a rush of questions immediately ensued. The island piqued the interest of people all over the world and stirred the fantasies of generations of archaeologists, researchers and the just plain curious, and continues to do so today.

I am one of the latter. From a very young age, I have had an extraordinary interest in **Rapa Nui**, which has brought me to visit the island on several occasions. I wanted to capture the wonder of the island in photographs and then publish them in a book. However, I lacked a sound text to support the pictures. The text had to be written by a specialist, an archaeologist perhaps. At the same time it had to be someone with close ties to **Rapa Nui**; if possible, someone who had lived there for many years.

All of these requirements were fulfilled when I met José Miguel Ramírez.

At that moment, the book began to take shape.

Carlos Huber

Introduction
A Unique Story

Rapa Nui is located at the easternmost vertex of the large triangular archipelago known as Polynesia. At the northernmost vertex lies Hawaii, with New Zealand marking the southwestern point. Over a two-thousand-year period, groups of navigators from Southeast Asia developed what is known as the Ancient Polynesian Culture, which was shared by hundreds of groups settling in the countless islands of the archipelago. The way the different settlements adapted to the various environmental conditions of the many islands resulted, over time, in a variety of social and cultural expressions.

The island of **Rapa Nui** is extremely isolated, being the point farthest removed from any other populated location on earth. As a result, its Polynesian roots, though recognizable, have evolved to unheard of extremes. The best known manifestations of the **Rapanui** historical and cultural development are the island's famous monolithic statues (**moai**), its megalithic altars (**ahu**), and a hieroglyphic type of writing (**rongo rongo**), which has yet to be deciphered, along with an advanced knowledge of engineering and astronomy. These achievements were the result of a complex process in which the particular environmental conditions interacted with a society driven by competition to gain prestige, to produce chiefs considered demigods, a religious aristocracy, and an ideology focused on ancestor worship. Warriors, priests, wise men (**maori**), specialized craftsmen, farmers, and servants were other members of the society.

The true "mystery" of the island lies not so much in the **moai** statues and the techniques used to transport them, a feat of engineering present in many cultures around the world, but rather the paradox of how, within the context of the overall development of humanity, this complex culture could emerge under such isolated conditions. Normally, high cultures or civilizations developed in places with favorable conditions for food production, where a relatively large population came easily into contact with other populations, whereby the resulting exchange of ideas and products facilitated new cultural advances. The knowledge we have of what happened on this island breaks all the rules. However, it is possible that the island was not as isolated as once believed, and that the environment was not as poor as previously thought.

Rapa Nui, or Big **Rapa**, was given its present name by European sailors visiting this part of the South Pacific, based on a perceived resemblance with the island **Rapa Iti** (Little **Rapa**), located 5,000 kilometers to the west. The islanders have now adopted the

MATAVERI AIRPORT, WITH A LANDING STRIP LARGE ENOUGH FOR A SPACE SHUTTLE TO LAND ON

name of **Rapa Nui** for their island and culture. Names worthy of note other than those reported by visiting mariners are the traditional **Te Pito O Te Henua** (the Navel of the World) and something similar recorded in an old manuscript, **Te Pito O Te Kainga** (the Center of Mother Earth). The name used in official texts is Easter Island, a name given by the Dutch Captain Jacob Roggeveen who discovered it on Easter Sunday, April 5, 1722.

From that time on, the image of an island full of mysteries began to spread. One reason was because the island's desolate landscape appeared to be the worst conceivable setting for the development of a complex society with monumental expressions similar to those of a high culture of the pre-Columbian Americas or the Old World.

The logs of the Dutch, who went ashore for a few hours, record the existence of enormous statues, as well as a lack of trees and rope material for their construction and movement, which prompted them to think that the figures were made of clay covered with stone incrustations.

The purported mysteries of the island were upheld in good measure by the fact that the islanders themselves came very close to extermination. During the eighteenth century, contacts with Western civilization were scant and short-lived. Forty-eight years after being discovered by the Dutch, the Spanish Captain Felipe González y Aedo arrived. In 1774, the famous English Captain James Cook landed, accompanied by the Forsters, who were German naturalists, and the painter Hodges, leaving valuable testimonies of the island in those days. In 1786, the French Admiral Jean François de Galaup, Count of La Pérouse, visited the island for 24 hours and left seeds and animals for the islanders' agriculture. These were immediately eaten by the natives. The Admiral also left many descriptions of the island.

These initial contacts proved to be of little importance for the island and the survival of the population and its culture. However, the nineteenth century was to mark the onset of many negative impacts that would lead to the loss of a great deal of information about the island's past, its traditions and ancient forms of organization, its rites and ceremonies.

In 1805, a passing American galley kidnapped a dozen men and women to be used as labor for seal hunts in the Juan Fernandez Islands. In late 1862, an international slave-hunting expedition was organized on the island, leading to the forced removal of a large part of the population, including the heirs of the ancient aristocracy and many of the wise men. The incident severely affected island culture and society. It is estimated that around 2,000 islanders were taken to Peru as slaves. The few survivors who did return to the island brought with them smallpox and tuberculosis, fatal diseases for the defenseless population.

In 1864, in the midst of this disaster, the first Catholic missionary, Brother Eugene Eyraud, arrived from Chile. Although not well received by the islanders, he set the groundwork for the arrival of other missionaries. After a year of evangelical work, he was almost forcibly rescued, but returned later with the first group of priests in 1866 to build the first Catholic mission at **Hanga Roa**.

The arrival from Tahiti in 1868 of Dutroux-Bornier, a French adventurer who gained control of the islanders through trickery, in association with John Brander, a rich English merchant, finally caused the withdrawal of the priests to French Polynesia in 1870, accompanied by a substantial number of refugees. This latest incident brought the native population on the island down to 111 survivors, according to 1877 records, a dramatically low number in comparison to the population estimated at 6,000 at the time of its first contact with Europeans.

Added to this loss was the pillage of several pieces of the island's archaeological heritage, such as the **moai** taken from **Orongo** by sailors of the English warship Topaze in 1868. This exceptional basalt statue, named **Hoa Haka Nana Ia**, has since been on display at the British Museum. It is believed that the last **tangata manu** (birdman) ceremony was performed at **Orongo**, a short time before the removal of the statue.

The excesses of Dutroux-Bornier led to his assassination at the hands of the islanders in 1877, but not before he had left behind numerous descendents who were to be the founders of two island lineages continuing on down to present times (**Paoa** and **Araki**). His successor, Alexander Salmon, of royal Tahitian descent on his mother's side, also instituted cultural changes while he lived on the island. These changes included trade in traditional art, the raising of sheep and cattle, and the influence of the Tahitian language and culture.

Around this time, probably starting with his voyages to the island as a midshipman in 1870, as lieutenant in 1875, and thereafter as the commander of the corvette Abtao, the naval Captain Policarpo Toro began to make arrangements for an initiative to annex the island to Chile.

Toro obtained the support of the Chilean government to purchase the landholdings from the Catholic mission of Tahiti, the Salmon brothers, John Brander Jr., and the natives.

Finally, upon returning to the island on September 9, 1888, Toro arranged for the transfer of sovereignty by the **Rapanui** chiefs, led by the **Ariki Atamu Tekena**. In this agreement, the islanders ceded sovereignty to Chile but retained their investitures. At that time, the island had about 200 inhabitants.

In 1895, the government-owned portion of the island was leased to a French merchant living in Valparaíso, Enrique Merlet, who in 1903 became head of the Easter Island Exploitation Company, thereafter known as Williamson & Balfour.

The islanders were restricted to **Hanga Roa**, still the only population center today. They were made to work for the company as peasants. The island was reduced to a single enormous livestock ranch, which ultimately numbered around 60,000 head of sheep. This was doubtlessly the most sorrowful period for the few remaining descendents of the proud **Rapanui** society.

The defenselessness of the islanders against the abuses of the company was witnessed by few during the first half of the twentieth century. One of the most important observers, however, was Katherine Routledge, an Englishwoman who lived on the island for 16 months and gathered a substantial amount of information on its customs, legends, and language. She even excavated alongside the **Rano Raraku moai**. *In 1914, she was a witness to a rebellion against the company led by María* **Angata**.

It was not until 1916 that the island was incorporated as an administrative district of Chilean territory, annexed to the province of Valparaíso. As a result of conflicts with the company, the island was officially registered as government property in 1933.

In 1934, the first scientific mission was established on the island. This was a Franco-Belgian expedition headed by the renowned anthropologist Alfred Mètraux, author of the principal work on **Rapanui** ethnology, and Henri Lavachery, who dedicated himself to the study of petroglyphs. In 1935, the entire island was declared a national park for tourism and a historic monument, in order to protect the archaeological monuments and preserve the **toromiro** trees.

In 1936, the Apostolic Vicariate of the Araucanía region of Chile took charge of the Church on the island. The first priest, a Capuchin, was Father Sebastian Englert, who dedicated much of his life to the study of **Rapanui** traditions and language. He was entrusted with conducting the first archaeological inventory on the island.

At the time of his death in 1969, he was considered the "uncrowned king" of the island.

Annual reports by the Chilean Navy and complaints from the Church finally caused the revocation of the contract with the company in 1953. The island was then placed under the guardianship of the Chilean Navy until civilian administration was set up in 1966. Alfonso Rapu, a young **Rapanui** teacher, became the leader who motivated the change.

Systematic archaeological work had begun in 1955 with the extraordinary expedition organized by Thor Heyerdahl, which restored the image of splendor of the ancient island culture. This was not only especially important for its direct heirs, but for the outside world as well. The reconstruction of monumental sites and the opening up to international tourism have been the key to restoring the islanders' self-esteem and their pride in their culture and past,

along with the contradictions that are inherent in a progressive process of acculturation and change.

It could well be asserted that the phenomenon of the **Rapanui** culture is a living paradox. It is surprising not merely because of its manifestations of a remote past, but also for the extraordinary ability to adapt, invent, and survive exhibited by a small population subjected to so many extreme internal and external impacts in recent centuries.

The first air contact with the island was in 1951, an extraordinary feat by Chilean Air Force Commander Roberto Parragué. Piloting the Catalina hydroplane **Manutara**, Parragué flew the distance separating La Serena and the island in 19 hours. An air route including Tahiti was inaugurated in 1965 by Parragué himself. The first commercial flight was made by a Lan Chile Airline DC-6 in 1967, landing on a dirt runway handmade by the islanders themselves. This officially opened the island to tourism.

Among the archaeologists invited by Heyerdahl was William Mulloy, an American who would initiate the monumental restoration work on the island. During the 1955-56 expedition, the first **moai** at **Ahu Ature Huki** at **Anakena** (page 99) was placed upright (all the **moai** were overturned at that time) under the leadership of Pedro Atan, then the mayor of the island.

On his return to the island in 1960, Mulloy directed the restoration of **Ahu Akivi** (page 106) together with Gonzalo Figueroa, a Chilean archaeologist who had also participated in Heyerdahl's expedition. Archaeologist William Ayres then joined Mulloy's work of restoring the **Tahai** Ceremonial Complex (page 59) between 1968-1970. In 1972, Mulloy restored **Ahu Hanga Kio'e**, located to the north of **Tahai**, and **Ahu Huri A Urenga** (page 111), an inland **ahu** with a precise astronomical orientation.

Mulloy began work on another small **ahu** situated nearby in 1976, but this was finished by Figueroa and the islander archaeologist Sergio Rapu. Between 1974 and 1976, Mulloy directed the restoration of the **Orongo** Ceremonial Village (page 39). Mulloy died in 1978, and his ashes were placed beneath a monolith near the **Tahai** Complex in recognition of his important contribution to the **Rapanui** culture and his outstanding human qualities.

Between 1979 and 1980, Sergio Rapu, working together with Andrea Seelenfreund, a Chilean archaeologist, and Charles Love, restored **Ahu Tautira**, or **Ko Peka Tae Ati**, in the **Hanga Roa** cove area across from the soccer field.

One of the most interesting restorations was done by Sergio Rapu at **Ahu Nau Nau** (page 96) at **Anakena** between 1978 and 1980. Along with the beautiful construction details of the different extensions of the monument of the **Ariki Henua** (High Chief of the island), a **moai** eye (page 56) carved out of white coral with a disc of red scoria was discovered for the first time, by Sonia Haoa.

This was the expression of the living face (**aringa ora**) of the ancestors and of the force of **mana**, systematically destroyed later on during the wars. It is now on display at the Padre Sebastian Englert Anthropological Museum near **Tahai**.

In recent years, a private Japanese company contributed major funding and a crane for the restoration of the largest monument erected in ancient times, **Ahu Tongariki** (page 81). This enormous platform, 150 meters long with 15 large **moai**, had been destroyed in the civil wars, leaving the **moai** toppled over onto the platform. The 1960 tsunami scattered these giant blocks of stone over an extensive area. The reconstruction work was commissioned to the Institute of Easter Island Studies of the University of Chile, under the direction of the archaeologist Claudio Cristino.

One of the most important (*albeit less spectacular*) tasks has been the inventory of archaeological sites begun by Father Englert. Systematic prospecting was resumed by archaeologist Patrick McCoy in 1968, and the institute continued his work. This project includes the documentation of petroglyphs by Dr. Georgia Lee beginning in 1981, and of statues and related items by Dr. Jo Anne Van Tilburg. Other archaeologists have been quietly at work on the island, with Dr. Christopher Stevenson being one of the most systematic among them.

Recently, archaeologists Sergio Rapu and José Miguel Ramírez took on the restoration of **Ahu Riata** at **Hanga Piko**.

In any event, the principal concern of professionals is the preservation and conservation of the cultural heritage through a sustainable development policy on land use and tourism. Among the sites at greatest risk is **Orongo**, due to the poor quality of the substrate in the area of the petroglyphs.

As archaeological tourism is the island's only industry, every effort must be made to keep the community's development needs compatible with the preservation of its heritage. **Rapa Nui** National Park was included on the World Heritage List in 1995 at the request of the Chilean government.

EUCALYPTUS GROVES AND VOLCANIC CONES

The Setting
A Changing Scenery

Rapa Nui is located 3,700 km off the coast of South America at subtropical latitude (27° 09' S Lat. and 109° 27' W Long). The nearest populated landfall is Pitcairn Island, once the refuge of the mutineers of the Bounty, 2,000 km to the southwest.

The 166 square kilometers of the island's scanty, triangular-shaped land area is dominated by the summit of a large volcanic complex rising up some 3,000 meters above the ocean floor, allowing a series of hills to peak above the water line to a maximum elevation of only 511 meters above sea level at **Maunga Terevaka**, the volcano that forms the northern point of the island.

Around 3 million years ago, a series of eruptive processes began building up the ocean floor, which later became the eastern end of the island, called **Poike** (pages 21 and 90). The southern vertex of the island, with its impressive caldera 1,500 meters in diameter, is known as **Rano Kau** (page 33). As time went by, until around 10,000 years ago, the sinuous surface of the island was molded by numerous volcanic secondary cones and fissures. The majority of the hills are made of volcanic ash and red scoria, with the notable exception of the famous volcano known as **Rano Raraku**, partly comprised of the volcanic tuff that was to be selected for the sculpting of most of the **moai**.

Due to this origin, the island abounds with all kinds of volcanic rocks, ranging from the soft red scoria used to sculpt the cylinders (**pukao**, page 84) that were placed like hats on some of the **moai**; the soft white trachyte used for handicrafts; to the harder, finer basalts used on ceremonial constructions or for making fine, polished adzes (**toki**, page 73); and the crystalline obsidian, the black volcanic glass that was used for making a variety of tools, and in particular the classic projectile points and hand axes with sharp edges and fine handles (**mata'a**).

The present-day morphology of the island is marked by the gentle hills

South coast of the Poike peninsula and Motu Marotiri

formed by numerous secondary cones and the pronounced marine erosion around the entire perimeter of the island, which has created steep cliffs and a jagged coastline around almost all the island, with only two beautiful exceptions: the pink coral sand beaches of **Ovahe** and **Anakena** (pages 94 and 95). Almost all of the island's surface is rock-covered, including basalt outcrops, recent lava flows (such as in the **Roiho** area on the west coast), or smaller pyroclastic rock masses uniformly dispersed by ancient eruptions. The exception is **Poike**, the eastern peninsula of the island, built up as a large volcano made up of successive layers of clayey soils and secondary outcrops of trachyte, another type of volcanic ash. The almost entire absence of stones there gave rise to the myth that it had been cleared in ancient times through the forced labor of a subjugated group whose rebellion finally brought about the extermination of the dominating group, within the confusing issue of the long ears and short ears.

There are no rivers because the soils are very permeable. The only natural reserves of rainwater are the **Rano Kau**, **Rano Raraku**, and **Rano Aroi** craters (page 103). There are also a number of springs near the coast, many of which issue forth slightly brackish water due to their proximity to the sea. The presence of deep ravines is proof that these streams at some time in a remote past must have been larger. Even today, after it rains it is possible to see waterfalls of a couple of meters in height form for a short while in some areas of the ravine that drains the **Rano Aroi** crater. In ravines such as this and at numerous caves opening up to the surface of the island, the prevailing moisture sustains the existence of a variety of endemic grasses and ferns in an environment that seems most exotic in comparison to the scant vegetation throughout most of the island, which at present is predominantly a steppe of hard grasses and introduced weeds, shrubs such as lupines and guavas, and a few groves of planted trees, such as eucalyptus.

The extreme isolation of **Rapa Nui** limited its population of plant and animal species, both land and marine. Even the variety and abundance of fish and shellfish is much less in comparison to other islands of Polynesia. Moreover, the subtropical location of the island, with its two well-defined seasons, unlike in the tropics, must have placed greater requirements on the adaptation of species as well as on the human colonizers themselves.

The data on the paleo-environment based on the evidence provided by fossilized pollen found in a sequence covering the last 38,000 years show a quite different island from today's. In some areas of the island, particularly on the hillsides, forest growths of woody species abounded, of which several types of extinct species have been recognized at different times: **toromiro** (Sophora

AHU TONGARIKI AND THE CRATER OF RANO RARAKU

toromiro); sandalwood (*Santalum sp.*); a type of palm tree with small coconuts (*Paschalococos disperta*) similar to a kind found in the central zone of Chile (*Jubaea chilensis*); a rubiaceous species and a conifer, both unknown; and thirteen recently identified new species, thus exhibiting an unsuspected floristic diversity. This composition corresponds to a humid environment with trees of considerable size, being very different from how the island looked to the Europeans who first came ashore in the early eighteenth century.

A few endemic species survive even today, such as the **hau hau** (*Triumfetta semitriloba*) and the **ngaoho** (*Caesalpinia major*). The **hau hau** yielded fibers for making ropes, and its wood was used to light fires by friction. Among the vegetal species present on the island since remote times is the totora (*Scirpus californicus*), a bulrush that grows in the freshwater ponds of the volcanic craters. Around 50 vegetal species have been identified that existed on the island before the arrival of man, including 12 varieties of ferns. Species that were economically important in the rest of Polynesia, such as the coconut palm (*Cocos nucifera*) and the breadfruit tree (*Artocarpus altilis*), did not arrive on the island until recent times.

The original wildlife fauna was basically made up of migratory birds, marine mammals, and fish. There were no land mammals on the island, and only a few insects and land snails present. Marine fauna in general must have served as the principal source of food for a time until the adaptation of introduced vegetal species was achieved. Fishing, although poor in comparison to that of the rest of Polynesia, must have been relatively accessible from the coastline and by watercraft, and would have been supplemented by the gathering of a few scant shellfish, algae, and crustaceans, such as lobsters. However, unlike many other islands in Polynesia, **Rapa Nui** lacked a coral reef that would have enormously facilitated access to the resources of the sea.

Recently, the remains of certain land

birds were identified that disappeared shortly after the arrival of the first human colonizers. Among these birds were two varieties of rail (Porzana sp.), two varieties of parrots, a type of heron, and an owl. Such migratory birds as albatrosses, fardelas, seagulls, frigate birds (page 43), tropical birds and others, can still be observed, although few in number and variety, in the islets lying off the coast of the southwest vertex of the island.

The native flora and fauna were enriched considerably with the arrival of the first Polynesian colonizers. In the very tradition related to the arrival of the **Ariki Hotu Matu'a**, there is a list of the plants of economic use brought in for establishment in the new land: bananas; a variety of tubers (taro, yam, sweet potatoes); sugar cane; gourds; shrubs of different uses, such as **mahute** (Broussonetia papyrifera) for making cloth; **ti** (Cordyline fruticosa) used as a foodstuff and for making dyes; **pua** (Curcuma longa) for pigments; **marikuru** (Sapindus saponaria), a white pigment for paint; and **mako'i** (Thespesia populnea), of considerable importance even today on account of the high quality of its wood.

Among the animals, chickens (**moa**) can be cited as an intentional introduction. The ancient Polynesians spread the use of pigs, dogs, and chickens all over the Pacific, but there is evidence of only chickens on **Rapa Nui**. Chickens played a predominant role in the economy and social life, to the point that veritable fortresses (**hare moa**) were eventually constructed to protect them. They were the means of exchange par excellence and a required offering at all ceremonies. Their white feathers were used in the brightest ornaments, especially in the headdresses of persons of high rank. The Polynesian mouse (**kio'e**), which ultimately was to multiply on a large scale, arrived as one of the transplanted species since it was a very important food resource. Two species of lizards (**moko**) also arrived with them.

The variety of vegetal species introduced in the new land, including more than 20 varieties of sweet potatoes (**kumara**), **taro**, and yam (**uhi**), demonstrates that a systematic, planned colonization was involved, rather than simply happenstance contact with a lost island in the midst of the ocean by a small group abandoned to its fate in a canoe either left to drift or driven randomly before storm winds. It would also not be logical to hold that this amounted to a single contact with the people involved, who thereafter remained in absolute isolation until historical times.

The presence on different islands in Polynesia of a South American crop such as the sweet potato, called by its Quechua name (**kumara**), opens up the issue of the human settlement of the island.

Aerial view of Rapa Nui, with Poike peninsula in the foreground

Ahu Vai Uri

THE ORIGINS
MYSTERY SOLVED?

All scientific evidence and traditions of **Rapa Nui** support a Polynesian origin for its inhabitants. However, the idea of an origin or influence from pre-Columbian America is still prevalent as an explanation to the historical and cultural development of the island.

One of the most widespread versions regarding the origins of the settlement in **Rapa Nui**, passed down as an oral tradition but with certain variations and evident contradictions, refers to the purported arrival of two migrations: the **Hanau Momoko** and, later, the **Hanau E'epe**. One of the best-known versions of the legend identifies **Ariki Hotu Matu'a** as the leader of the original expedition, acting as the head of the **Hanau Momoko**, while the **Hanau E'epe** are supposed to have

arrived in a second migration that came in from the east. The most common interpretation is that the former, the "short ears," were Polynesian and the possessors of a simple culture, while the latter, the "long ears," were from South America and supposedly imposed a complex culture that included the megalithism which was to characterize **Rapa Nui**. *Thor Heyerdahl, for his part, stubbornly insists that the island's first settlers were Americans belonging to some higher culture in pre-Columbian Peru, on the basis of scattered architectural data and other features of the Tiwanaku, Moche, and Inca cultures, mixing very distant locations and times.*

The first error springs from associating the name **Hanau E'epe** *with "long ear," based on the fact that in the* **Rapanui** *language "epe" means ear. However, "e'epe" actually means robust, while* **"momoko"** *means slender (literally, "lizard-like"). Thus, the names actually refer to two physical types, which remain recognizable today amongst the islanders, but which did not originate from migrations of people as different as the Polynesians and pre-Columbian Americans. The artificial lengthening of earlobes is a custom widely used throughout the world as a symbol of*

social rank. Besides, the presence of **"kumara"** (sweet potato) may be interpreted as proof of contact with South America, but evidence suggests that it was more likely brought back by Polynesian expeditions.

The achievement of a high degree of refinement in stone masonry, such as that occurring in some of the **Ahu**, is something that has appeared in many cultures throughout the world in which similar processes have taken place. Actual contact between cultures would have left its mark on many other aspects of the complex set of social and cultural elements as well, including biological traits.

In truth, nothing of what characterizes the complex developments of the Moche or Tiwanaku cultures has

been found on **Rapa Nui**. The only two pieces of "evidence" found by Heyerdahl in Tucume, a Moche complex in northern Perú, should be disregarded. His "birdman" holding an egg is a Moche bird holding something like an egg, and the double paddle is just a Moche paddle. In addition, we have the successful experiment recently accomplished by Hokule'a, which proved such contact was much easier than previously thought. The voyagers of this Hawaiian double-hulled canoe reached **Rapa Nui** on October 8, 1999, after a 1,500-mile, 17-day passage from Mangareva in French Polynesia.

Actually, what is observed on the island is a continuing developmental process, with no influences other than Polynesian. The archaeological, linguistic, anthropological, and biological evidence clearly links **Rapa Nui** with the center of Polynesia and, in particular, the Marquesas Islands. The monumental architecture itself is an outgrowth of a model used widely throughout Polynesia, where prototypes of the **Rapanui ahu** and **moai** are found, and in particular in the ideological and sociopolitical model that gives it its special character in time and space. The way this complex developed on **Rapa Nui** must be understood within the special environmental conditions that stimulated the process of adaptation to this newly colonized territory.

The origins of this complex were found some 3,000 years ago on Tonga and Samoa, the gateway to what was to become the **A**ncestral **P**olynesian **C**ulture. The expansion of navigator groups to the east required the development of special technologies and skills, combined with the extraordinary navigating capabilities the Polynesians were to demonstrate. They added efficient agricultural production systems

Anakena and *Ovahe* beach. Between them are **Maunga Hau Epa**, **Maunga Koua**, and **Maunga Puha Roa**.

of a religious and defensive type, and that even managed to rise above the level of chiefdoms, such as the kingdoms of Tonga and Hawaii, New Zealand and Tahiti.

The expansion towards the center of Polynesia, to the Society Islands and the Marquesas, most likely occurred a few centuries before the Christian era. Current data indicates that Hawaii was settled between 500 and 750 A.D., and New Zealand somewhat later, between 900 and 1000 A.D. This process was probably not linear, spreading from a single distribution point at the center of Polynesia. At a certain time, it appeared that an explosive phenomenon occurred which moved different groups to colonize an extremely vast territory out towards the boundaries of the Polynesian triangle, with possible contacts even beyond. Actually, a particular island was not a limit for a Polynesian sailor, but a starting point to continue on to other territories.

Their extraordinary marine technology and systematic knowledge of the sea and celestial phenomena gave the Polynesians a unique capability to colonize hundreds of islands separated by enormous distances. One of the mechanisms that they must have surely known, and which would have facilitated navigation to the east in order to reach such a remote place as **Rapa Nui**, is the El Niño phenomenon. Under such conditions, they could have reached the island and then continued on to South America. According to observed patterns, these winds could have brought them to the south-central coasts of Chile.

Among the Mapuche people occupying that area of Chile since

to their traditional exploitation of marine resources, which depended on the capacities of the different environments they occupied.

Agricultural production seems to be essential to the development of complex societies in which non-egalitarian stratification is associated with ideology, ancestor worship, rituals and monumental structures, scientific knowledge, the divine origin of chiefs and their supernatural power (**mana**), and thence their coercive capability to impose rules and taboos (**tapu**), as well as the maintenance and enhancement of their prestige through the largesse of a generous redistribution of surpluses.

In this process, there were societies that attained a high degree of refinement and complexity based on sustaining a high population density with sophisticated agricultural production systems and monumental constructions

pre-Spanish times, certain archaeological, linguistic and even biological elements have been described that could have derived from contact with Polynesian groups. These were artifacts such as a very special weapon, the Maori-type "**wahaika**" hand club, but made of locally-available slate instead of wood. Among the Mapuche, the term "**toki**" means a warrior chief, but can also refer to a polished stone axe head, this being a widespread term for adzes in Polynesia. In addition, Mapuche warrior chiefs used a symbol of rank called "**toki-kura**" made of polished stone with a hole for hanging it around the neck; both the word and the artifact clearly seem Maori-Mapuche matchings. Whether these matchings are borrowings due to some kind of contact or are independent developments remains an open issue.

A total of a dozen similar words

*could be evidence of contact, as well as the presence of Polynesian physical traits (rocker jaw) in individuals buried in pre-Spanish contexts in southern Chile. These included such common elements as underground cooking ovens (curanto on Chiloe island and **umu pae** in **Rapa Nui**), or the use of similar terms for reciprocity activities (**minga** on Chiloe, **mink'a** in Quechua, and **umanga** in **Rapa Nui**).*

*Archaeological evidence for the settling of **Rapa Nui** is not conclusive. The year 300 A.D. has been referred to as the initial date of settlement, based on linguistic extrapolations and an unreliable radiocarbon dating. Another date, around 700 A.D., supposedly associated with the first construction phase of a ceremonial structure in **Tahai**, on the west coast of the island, must be ruled out because the association with the monument is extremely doubtful.*

*However, the soundest evidence comes from a recent excavation at **Anakena**, where remains of extinct terrestrial birds have been found. The oldest recorded date is between 615 and 864 A.D. In this context, it has been noted that the first occupants based more of their sustenance on the hunting of marine mammals and birds than on fishing or raising chickens. The abundance of dolphin remains is evidence of the first colonizers' capability to access the resources of the high seas, while the presence of extinct terrestrial birds shows to what extent man affected the equilibrium of the ecosystem, without forgetting the probable catastrophic impact of cyclic phenomena such as El Niño or the Little Ice Age that occurred between the thirteenth and fourteenth centuries.*

During this period, the island underwent a process of severe environmental deterioration that is inevitable when a small, fragile environment is combined with a society oriented towards competition, progressively intensifying the pressure on limited resources. Within this scenario, one of the most critical factors

ANAKENA BEACH

was the number of inhabitants the island might have been eventually able to support (carrying capacity). The most conservative estimates indicate that the population peaked at 10,000 inhabitants. At least certain data given by the first European visitors gave accounts of figures of as many as 6,000 inhabitants. Currently, some 3,000 people live on the island.

The arboreal vegetation was intensely affected due to its important use in large public and ceremonial works, as well as for firewood for daily consumption, and by a slash and burn type of agriculture, i.e., cutting down and burning forest areas to plant tubers. It should also be noted that the ancient practice of cremation consumed large amounts of wood.

TONGARIKI AT DAWN

*This occurred progressively on the island until, towards the seventeenth century, the ecological disaster of deforestation eliminated the raw material necessary for making ocean-going craft, and hence brought about the impossibility of reducing the pressure on the environment through the emigration of a part of the population, which was one of the mechanisms that had stimulated the discovery and colonization of so many islands in the Pacific. All of the other activities that in large part depended on such resources, such as the construction of **ahu** and the transportation of **moai**, must surely have also been affected. The radical change in burial practices shows how deeply the whole society was affected and its impressive ability to adapt.*

The Origins Revisited

One of the most interesting versions of the oral tradition concerning the discovery and settlement of **Rapa Nui** is found in a manuscript from the early twentieth century. The so-called Manuscript E, or "The Traditions of **Pua Ara Hoa**", was found on the island by the German scholar Thomas Barthel in 1956.

This little-known source, the most important account of the **Rapanui** tradition written down in **Rapanui**, describes in greater detail the classic but confused subject of **Hotu Matu'a**.

The first discovery here is the name **Hotu A Matu'a** (**Hotu**, son of **Matu'a**) and his position as the tenth "**Ariki motongi**" in a genealogy starting with **Oto Uta**, whose broken statue (**moai**) was finally brought to the new land in one of the subsequent voyages back and forth to **Hiva**, the homeland.

Then it explains the situation that led to the departure from the ancestral lands in a territory named "**Marae Renga**", in **Hiva**. The ancient wise men (**maori**) had predicted that there would come a time in which the earth would sink, and this began to occur in the time of the fourth **Ariki**. The rising waters took many lives, and in the following generations canoes were built to escape.

The episode known as **Haumaka**'s dream occurred in the time of **Ariki Matu'a**, the father of **Hotu**. In this dream, **Haumaka**'s spirit traveled towards the rising sun in search of a new land. Finally, the spirit descended on the islets located near the southwest vertex of the new land, which it identifies as the three children of **Ariki Taanga** (the grandfather of **Hotu Matua'a**) turned into stone (**Motu Kao Kao, Motu Iti**, and **Motu Nui**). The spirit traveled along the southern and northern coasts until reaching the best place for landing: the Bay of the Shining Sand (**Hanga Mori A One**), which is known today by the name of **Anakena**.

Before returning from this "astral journey", the spirit named the island "**Te Pito O Te Kainga**".

Seven explorers were sent out to the new land. They were able to recognize the sites described by **Haumaka**. Among much of the classic but more detailed information recorded in the manuscript, there is reference to another inhabitant they found on the island (**Nga Tavake**), who told them he had arrived with yet another person, who had since died (**Te Ohiro**).

Back in the homeland of **Hiva**, in the time of **Ariki Matu'a**, the religious leader of the **Hanau momoko**, their neighbors **Hanau e'epe** usurped part of their lands by removing their boundaries because of the rising waters of the sea which had killed many of them.

The usurping **Hanau e'epe** were dominated and finally transported to the new land as prisoners. After arriving on the island, the **Ariki Hotu A Matu'a** settled them in the **Poike** area and assigned them their own chief.

There is no reference to long and short ears, which can definitely be considered as a misinterpretation, but to a common Polynesian origin of two closely related groups.

The manuscript refers to more than one trip of settlement, something that fits much better with scientific evidence and common sense.

TONGARIKI (*above*)
RANO RARAKU (*below*)

Organization of the Ancient Society

Based on the legend of **Ariki Hotu A Matu'a**, a social order was established headed by the royal family (**ariki paka**) and the religious aristocracy, including the wise men (**maori**) and priests (**ivi atua**), and beneath them a variety of artisan specialists, warriors (**matato'a**), fishermen (**tangata tere vaka**), and farmers (**tangata keu keu henua**). At the lower level were servants (**kio**) and defeated enemies to be sacrificed (**ika**).

The position of the aristocracy was upheld through claims of divine origin as descendents of the gods of creation.

In the lines of descent of the **Ariki** of **Rapa Nui** within the **Honga** lineage of the **Miru** clan, the firstborn son was destined to receive power as the religious leader of the island. The important men, such as the **Ariki**, were invested with a power of supernatural origin, called **mana**, and were protected by the rules of **tapu**, or taboo. This power was concentrated in a person's head, which according to tradition was not to be touched by anyone. Even the hair on such a person's head was not to be cut. This power could be expressed positively, at times of initiating plantings or harvests, or negatively, even causing death.

The control of food production translated into an intensification of agricultural output, which provided the islanders' subsistence, while the most coveted kinds of seafood, such as tuna fish and turtles, were reserved for nobility. Such items were harvested from the sea by certain specialists commissioned for this purpose and were subject to taboo restrictions during several months of the year. Major festivals and ceremonies were occasions for the redistribution of food, which was one of the characteristic elements of societies such as the **Rapa Nui**, organized as chiefdoms.

The greater or lesser importance of people in the social pyramid was structured in terms of the degree of closeness held in relationship with their most important ancestor. This became more and more complicated over time as the population increased and families (**ure**), lineages (**paenga**), and clans (**mata**) were subdivided or merged depending on historical circumstances. Cases of conflict in which a family was taken over by a more powerful group was common. Cases similar to these

island's late prehistoric period, eight major and four minor clans were recognized. These were organized into two large confederations that divided the island into two parts: the clans associated with the **Miru**, the royal lineage, who lived on the northwestern half of the island (**Ko Tu'u Aro**), and those who occupied the southeastern half, grouped under the name of **Hotu Iti**.

In this context, the monumental constructions dedicated to the worship of each lineage's founding ancestors constituted the visible evidence of genealogical ties to the land. At the same time, they legitimized the ownership of the land and made permanent reference to the **mana** of the ancestors incarnate in each image (**moai**), which were the living countenance (**aringa ora**) of some clearly identified ancestor.

The centers of this political and religious power were located on the coast, to control independent, autonomous territories (**kainga**) which extended inland onto the island. Land boundaries were marked by piles of stones (**pipi horeko**), and trespassing was normally considered a serious offense, even punishable by death. Elite members and priests lived near the **ahu** in houses shaped like overturned boats (**hare paenga** or **hare vaka**). Farther inland, families gathered around their most important male relative (**tangata honui**), generally elders that headed the lineages. These families established small permanent or semi-permanent settlements alongside the crop fields. These dwellings were less elaborate:

ultimately led to the establishment of two confederations of clans.

According to tradition, before dying, **Ariki Hotu A Matu'a** divided the island among his sons, who finally formed their own clans. The firstborn, **Tu'u Maheke**, received the land between **Anakena** and **Maunga Tea Tea**; **Miru**, received the land between **Anakena** and **Hanga Roa**; the third son, **Marama**, the territory between **Akahanga** and **Vinapu**; **Ra'a** inherited the area located to the north and west of **Maunga Tea Tea**; **Koro Orongo**, the territory between **Anakena** and the volcano **Rano Raraku**; and the last son, **Hotu Iti**, the eastern portion of the island. In the

besides the elliptical structures such as the **hare paenga**, houses were laid out on rectangular and circular plans. The household architecture was completed by underground hearths bounded by basalt slabs (**umu pae**, page 54), and in the Late Period, by chicken coops (**hare moa**) and circular structures for the protection of plants (**manavai**, page 55).

There probably existed common access areas for the exploitation of certain resources, such as quarries or forests with special characteristics. The control of some of these resources by different groups must have encouraged the maintenance of rules of reciprocity and exchange.

The crater of Rano Kau

Aerial view of Orongo village and Rano Kau crater

CRISIS AND ADAPTATION

THE HURI-MOAI PHASE
(1680-1867 A.D.)

In the traditional framework for the historical and cultural development of **Rapa Nui**, the events characterized by the **Huri-Moai** phase, the toppling of the statues, took place around 1680 A.D., which would coincide with the tradition regarding the battle of **Poike**. According to this legend, the **Hanau e'epe** (the "long ear" of the confusing version), were almost completely annihilated in that event as the result of a final rebellion to overthrow the dominant class. A long ditch at the base of **Poike**, which was supposed to represent "the big cooking oven of the **Hanau e'epe**" (**Ko Te Umu O Te Hanau e'epe**), was something different.

Even though the abandonment of megalithism appears to have occurred suddenly, in a manner similar to that in which legend tells of a powerful woman who ordered the toppling of the statues in revenge for not receiving her share of an enormous lobster, the process was in truth one of a cumulative nature involving a number of factors, in which adaptation to new, critical conditions was necessarily a relatively prolonged process over time.

This process must have started at least around the year 1500, expressed then as a series of conflicts between neighboring groups, warfare that brought about the destruction of the **ahu** and the **moai** of the vanquished. In this context, the prestige of the priestly class waned before the waxing hegemony of the warrior class (**matato'a**). The food production crisis made it necessary to reduce the pressure on the environment through the use of a less demanding economic system along with more conservative, efficient technologies for the protection of plants. Ceremonies were oriented towards ensuring fertility and using the magic of **mana** to influence the resources required for subsistence.

Throughout this period and on down to historical times, all of the **moai** on the island were overturned. The figures' **mana** was eliminated through the removal and destruction of their coral eyes. The **ahu** were transformed and their original shape hidden, and chambers (**avanga**) were constructed inside to receive the bleached bones of the ancient families, probably as an adaptation to the lack of trees providing wood for fuel. This continuity in the use of old power centers indicates that this was no simple usurpation by enemy groups, but that the owners themselves destroyed the statues after losing the underpinnings of the traditional system.

The efforts to maintain the system through making greater demands on the population and resources must have brought dramatic tensions into play. The

gigantic **moai** abandoned in the quarry demonstrate a need to cling to the **mana** of the ancestors to an extent that was simply impossible to maintain.

The deterioration of the environment made it necessary to look for more efficient alternatives. Among the technological developments were circular stone enclosures, called **manavai**, built above- or underground where natural hollows could be used to shelter plants from the wind and loss of moisture. Chickens were protected by means of veritable stone fortresses used as chicken coops (**hare moa**). Covering the soil with rocks (mulching) served the same purpose.

From an ideological point of view, the rites of the first fruits and the magic of fertility took on greater importance. Many artifacts charged with **mana** were earmarked as favoring the growth of plants, the fertility of chickens, and luck in fishing. One of these magic stones, named **Te Pu O Hiro** (**Hiro**'s trumpet), had holes that were blown through, making a sound that was thought to attract schools of fish towards the shore. This and many other stones were engraved with fine lines representing **komari** (vulva), the traditional fertility symbol. This is the period which most likely corresponds to the majority of the petroglyphs depicting **komari**, fish, birds, and plants. The skulls of important persons were even removed from ossuaries to allow the **mana** they purportedly possessed to be put to use for such purposes.

The most notable expression of these adaptations can be found in the realm of ideology, in the worship of **Make Make** (the "creator god"), and the ceremony of the **tangata manu** (birdman). The ancient worship of ancestors at each family's religious center gave way to annual competitions for power held at the ceremonial center in the village of **Orongo**.

The motu (islets) and the caldera of Rano Kau

ORONGO
SITE OF THE TANGATA MANU COMPETITION

The ceremonial village of **Orongo** is located on the narrowest edge of **Rano Kau** in one of the most spectacular settings on the island. The basin of the crater is nearly a kilometer and a half in diameter, and rainwater has filled it to form a reed-covered lake.

The interior of the crater, with its 200-meter high walls, is a huge natural **manavai** (garden enclosure), with a microclimate in which the native plant species and those brought by the Polynesian colonizers thrive. In fact, the last **toromiro** tree was still clinging to the rocky slopes until 1960. Past generations have planted inside the crater exotic trees and bushes that now dominate several areas, including avocado trees and **miro tahiti**. There are even some wild grapevines and a huge pink bougainvillea at the foot of the **kari kari**.

Besides the main project with **toromiro**, Conaf is working to increase the population of the few remaining specimens of the small native **hau hau** and **marikuru** trees.

The lake was one of the main sources of water for the **Hanga Roa** population until some 30 years ago. A record of the names given to the different "eyes of water" is still kept, and the legendary name of this crater is **Te Poko Uri A Haumaka O Hiva** (The Black Abyss of **Haumaka** from **Hiva**).

Laminate slabs of basalt called **keho** abound on the edge of the crater. This stone was used to build the village of **Orongo**, which dominated the southwest edge of the crater, to the side of the eroded notch, called **kari kari**, across from the islets (**motu**).

The first buildings were probably not related to the birdman cult. In fact, just outside the village one can see the remains of a small **ahu**, and from its **moai**, sculpted from the **Rano Raraku** tuff, only the ground-level base remains. Across from the **ahu**, there are orifices in the rocks that may have been used for astronomical purposes. The first stone houses in **Orongo** seem to have been built during the **Ahu-Moai** phase, around 1200 A.D. Near the stone outcrop located at what would now be the center of the village, the first houses were built with an elongated oval-shaped floor.

Basalt slabs were placed on these to form thick walls filled with gravel and rocks, and longer slabs were then placed above to form a false vault roof. A thick filling over the vault is what gave the buildings stability. Only a small door

A PARTIAL VIEW OF THE TANGATA MANU COMPETITION SETTING

could be used in these structures so that the occupant had to enter on hands and knees. This was located at the front of the house, which always faced the sea. The lack of windows meant the houses were quite dark and allowed for little air circulation.

They were only used at certain times of the year, for sleeping. As time passed by, and especially in connection with the **tangata-manu** ceremony, which became important during the second phase of the island's prehistory, 53 houses were built, lined up along the edge of the crater, forming three separate but harmonious groups of buildings. Almost all of the houses were ransacked and destroyed during the island's recorded history, and have been rebuilt several times in the last 20 years. At the entrance to the village, two houses near the cliff were left intentionally unrestored so that they could be viewed in their natural state.

The first house of the first group was left open so that the shape, the thickness of the walls, and the false vault would be visible. The low ceilings do not allow the visitor to stand upright inside, and there is no light other than that which filters through the small entrances, of which there is frequently only one, and that quite small. The shape of the buildings and the type of construction makes them damp, and with no stabilizing materials other than the earth and gravel filling, the walls are very unstable, so that they must be repaired periodically. The floor plan of the houses is similar to that of boat-shaped houses.

These houses were built with solid walls instead of the light **hare vaka** roofs because the site is exposed to stiff winds coming off the ocean. The availability of the basalt slabs as a building material and the use of this simpler construction technique resulted in a group of dwellings with an architectural design that is unique on the island. Basalt blocks were used in

Aerial view of Orongo

1 **Mata Ngarau**, the area in which the **Tangata Manu** ceremony was held, concentrates the largest number of petroglyphs on the island.
2 The location of the first houses, which later became the village of **Orongo**.
3 The crater lake, covered with reeds (**nga'atu**). The 1.5-kilometer-wide crater is a large natural nursery for plants and trees.
4 **Taura Renga**, the house where the famous **Moai Hoa Haka Nana Ia** was located, a ceremonial and ritual center.
5 A house open on one end to show the details of the construction. The base, elliptical in shape, is 2 meters wide, 8 meters long, and 1.5 meters tall.

Orongo ceremonial village

The entrance to a house in Orongo

RECREATION OF THE TANGATA MANU CEREMONY

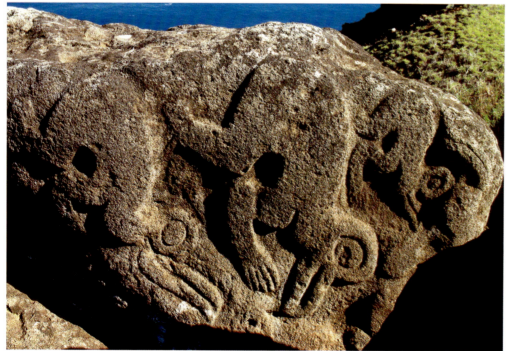

THE CLASSICAL DESIGN OF THE TANGATA MANU IN BAS-RELIEF

some walls, especially in the narrow doors, recycled from the older **hare paenga** foundations. Inside some of the houses several of the vertical slabs serving as interior wall foundations were painted with designs from the birdman ceremony, as well as with representations of European ships, proof that the dwellings were in use during the period of the island's recorded history. We do know for certain that the **tangata manu** ceremony was celebrated until the second half of the last century, around 1867.

One of the most impressive aspects of the village was the basalt **moai** called **Hoa Haka Nana Ia** (page 119). This **moai** is unique not only because it was sculpted from basalt, the hardest material available, but also because it represents both the change and continuity that was taking place in the ancient culture. The front side of the statue has the classical shape that flourished during the megalithic period, and carved on the back are all of the motifs that represent the second phase: **tangata manu** (birdman), **ao** (double-bladed paddle, a symbol of power), and **komari** (vulva, a fertility symbol).

RAPA NUI

MATA NGARAU

*Heading down toward the **kari kari**, the last group of houses is built against a natural outcrop of rocks almost completely covered with carvings, particularly of images in bas-relief of the **tangata manu**, the mask that represents the creator god **Make Make**, **komari**, and some geometric designs. This area, called **Mata Ngarau**, has the greatest concentration of petroglyphs on the island and was a ceremonial center. Six individual chambers were built in the center of the outcrop, where the priests awaited a signal from the competitors. On the other side of the outcrop, at the south end of the complex, a single large chamber marked the end of the village.*

GROUP OF PETROGLYPHS OF THE AREA

MATA NGARAU

The Motu
Manutara's Ancient Kingdom

The **Mata Ngarau** complex looks out over the islets where the main part of the competition for the search for the **manutara** egg took place. The islets **Motu Kao Kao**, **Motu Iti**, and **Motu Nui** are located about a kilometer away from the base of the cliff. A wide variety of sea birds would arrive to nest each spring, of which only a few now remain. Among the most important is the "frigate bird" (**makohe**), which can be seen gliding alone or occasionally in impressively large flocks. The famous **manutara**, a slate-colored sooty tern (*Sterna fuscata*) can no longer be found on the island.

Motu Kao Kao, the closest islet, is an imposing-looking, needle-shaped projection and a safe nesting place for the birds. **Motu Iti** lies a little farther out, a small flat islet with an obsidian quarry that was exploited in prehistoric times. The largest islet, **Motu Nui**, is separated from **Motu Iti** by a small channel, and is home to important archaeological remains related to the competition. The representatives (**hopu manu**) of each group would take refuge in caves, in which they left carvings and paintings such as the imposing red-painted face of **Make Make**. One of the most interesting relics, a small **moai** brought from **Rano Raraku**, is no longer on the islet. Tradition holds that this statue once marked the mid-section of the island across its center, dividing the territories of the two confederations of clans that dominated the last stage prior to the decadence of the historical period. An outcrop called **Puku Rangi Manu** is located at one end of **Motu Nui**, the place where the competitor who found the egg would announce his victory to the priests and chiefs waiting in **Orongo**.

Although details are few as to how the birdman competition came into being, we know at least that the name is related to a figure common in stone carvings, a profile of a bird-headed human figure curled up in the fetal position. The head is of the **makohe** bird rather than the **manutara**. According to tradition, once the ancestral cult that the **moai** represented fell from favor, and given the old religious-political order's loss of prestige, the warrior leaders came into power, bringing with them new rites oriented more towards fertility which were less labor- and resource-intensive. However, this brought about a need to define political power no longer through heredity, but through a selection process determined by the ritual competition held each spring. By the end of the 17th century, these changes in society led to the formation of two large confederations of clans which covered the northwest and southeast territories, respectively.

As springtime approached, the most powerful groups got together to participate in the competition. They would meet in the large village of **Mataveri** and, when the time was right, would go up to **Orongo**. Each clan chose a representative, the **hopu manu**. At the height of the festivities and rituals, the representative would climb down the **Orongo** cliff and swim out to **Motu Nui**, aided by reed (totora) floats, called **pora**. There they

would await the arrival of the sea birds until one of them was able to take possession of the first **manutara** egg. The victor would announce his triumph to his clan, whose chief would immediately become the one chosen by **Make Make** to be the **tangata manu** until the next spring. The **hopu manu** would return to the village with the intact egg, which represented the power of **Make Make**.

The recipient of this **mana**, the new leader, was anointed with the symbols of his new status. He was required to completely shave his head and was painted with the ritual colors of red and white. He would receive the **Ao**, the symbol of power, and finally, would begin the procession down the **Ao** road to **Mataveri**. While we do not know the details of the festivities and rituals, we know that the new chief would go into seclusion for about six months in **Anakena** if he belonged to the northwest clan (**Mata Tu'u Aro**), or in **Rano Raraku** if he was from the southeast (**Mata Hotu Iti**).

There was a special house prepared for this purpose, and the chief would be attended to by a single priest who would dedicate himself entirely to his service. The **mana** could be deadly if the rituals were not followed, but its power could ensure the privileges of the chief's clan and the magic of fertility to produce food. Tradition has it that the groups also took advantage of these privileges to assuage their lust for revenge. In fact, the bloodiest legends of the island are from this period, full of stories of cannibalism.

However, the islanders' search for political, ideological, and technical solutions to the crisis demonstrates their ability to adapt to change, so that we cannot refer to true cultural decadence in the civilization until it suffered the profound impact of contact with the Western world, which brought the population to the brink of extinction toward the end of the last century.

PAGE 43. *Above the **motu** and on the cliff of **Orongo**, flocks of frigate birds (**makohe**) can still be seen along with other migratory sea birds. The **manutara**, whose eggs played a crucial role in the **tangata manu** competition, has long since disappeared.*

SILHOUETTES OF MOTU KAO KAO AND THE CRATER OF RANO KAU VOLCANO, VIEWED FROM THE SEA

RANO KAU VOLCANO, IN THE MORNING

IN THE EVENIN

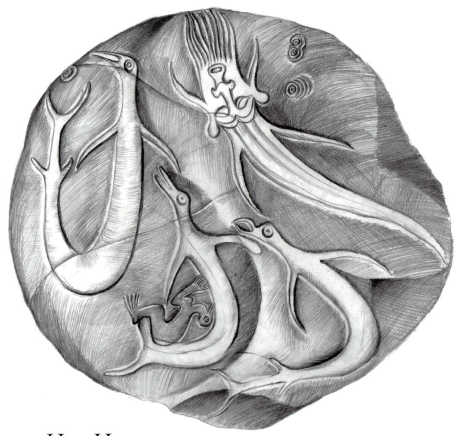

Hoa Hoka

*Beside the lagoon of the volcano **Rano Kau**, located on the north side of the crater, underneath the luxuriant foliage of the **miro tahiti**, there is an enormous block of rock, one of the island's ancient art masterpieces, that was carved with one of the most spectacular designs of **Rapa Nui** rock art. It displays stylized figures of eels, anthropomorphic faces representing spirits, and **tangata manu**.*

The crater of Rano Kau

Inland view from Rano Kau

ANA KAI TANGATA
CANNIBAL'S CAVE?

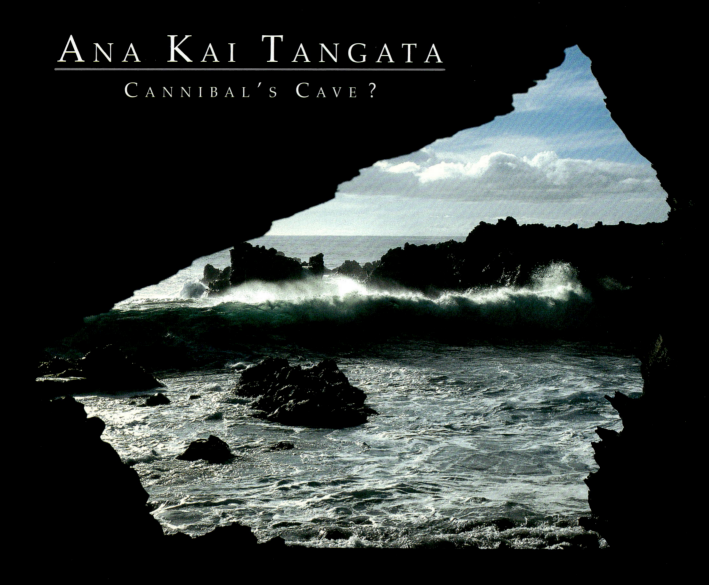

*The volcanic origin of the island, with its multiple, complex eruptive processes occurring over millions of years, fostered the formation of hundreds of caves (**ana**) at different depths throughout the island and all along the coast, like the big one (opposite page) close to **Ana Kai Tangata**, formed by a massive volcanic eruption over the ocean.*

*One of the most interesting caves is **Ana Kai Tangata** (above), a name erroneously translated as cannibal's cave, which still preserves some paintings related to the **tangata manu** ceremony. On a limited section of the high ceiling, figures of the **manutara** in red and white were painted on an irregular surface of basalt slabs. Because of moisture and the cracked structure of the slabs, many of them have already fallen down or have been vandalized, making its conservation a priority for it is a unique cultural patrimony.*

Hanga Roa village, as seen from the sea

Tahai ceremonial complex

Megalithic Culture

The Ahu-Moai Phase
(1000-1680 A.D.)

The Ahu

In Polynesia, as in many of the world's older civilizations, the ideology and power of the nobles found expression in the construction of monumental platforms built up progressively until taking on pyramidal shapes.

The basic forms were low, elongated stone platforms where images of ancestors or gods were erected, represented by means of simple vertical slabs of rock or coral, or figures carved in wood. This was laid out on the whole as a rectangular plaza, paved at times and completely walled in. Notable examples of these megalithic expressions are found throughout all of Polynesia,

as in the **marae** of the Society Islands, the **heiau** of Hawaii, the **me'ae** and **tohua** of the Marquesas Islands, the **tu'ahu** of New Zealand and, to an exceptional extent, the **ahu** of **Rapa Nui.**

In **Rapa Nui**, such platforms acquired new shapes through the incorporation of an inclined ramp at the front (**tahua**), paved with round stones taken from the coastal strip (**poro**) and provided with lateral extensions.

The selection of the site for the erection of an **ahu** must have been a matter not only for the engineering and architectural specialists (**tangata maori anga ahu**) to decide; it must surely have been also for the priests, whose job was to sanctify the place. This consecration was expressed by placing a layer of red scoria at the base.

The majority of the 272 **ahu** were erected along the coast, normally oriented parallel to the coastline. However, around 25 have been identified in which this was not the case. Of these, more than a third were oriented along lines according to precise astronomical observations. Of the **ahu** which were erected inland (around 30), two examples are notable: **Ahu Huri A Urenga** (page 111), oriented towards sunrise during the winter solstice, the shortest day of the austral year, around June 21; and **Ahu Akivi** (page 106), with its equinoctial orientation, in which the long axis of the **ahu** is oriented from north to south so as to be perfectly perpendicular to the axis of the sun in the autumn and spring equinoxes.

With time, each platform was to undergo a number of expansions, depending on the capacity of each group, eventually achieving refinements such

Ceremonial Place Details

1 PAENGA
2 TAUPEA
3 PORO

Hare Vaka or Hare Paenga

The houses (**hare**) for the aristocracy were in the shape of an inverted boat (**vaka**) demarcated by blocks of polished basalt (**paenga**). Branches placed in cylindrical openings held up the superstructure, made of light material (wood, branches, leaves, and grass).

The only entrance was a narrow opening in the center. The houses sometimes had an elaborate crescent-shaped pavement in the front (**taupea**) made of sea boulders (**poro**).

Inside, the floor was covered with dry grass and mats made of woven reeds (**peue and moenga**). The only furniture was stone pillows (**ngarua**), sometimes engraved with symbols.

Domestic utensils hung from the frame of the structure: gourds for holding all kinds of items, tools, cult objects, and the various small wooden statues.

Small stone statues embodying protective spirits were usually placed next to the door.

Engraved Stone Pillows

The **ngarua** are one of the household artifacts associated with the highest social rank, dreams, and magic. Some designs are of exceptional delicacy, carved into the hardest material, including symbols from the **rongo rongo** writing system. (Fonck Museum collection, Viña del Mar, Chile).

Umu Pae

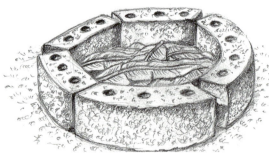

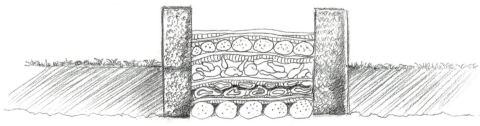

LEAVES
HEATED STONES
LEAVES
TUBERS (sweet potato, yam)
LEAVES
MEAT
LEAVES
HEATED STONES

Drawing of a Ceremonial Site

1 **Ahu**. Ceremonial platform
2 **Moai**. Ancestor's image
3 **Pukao**. Topknot
4 Cremation pit
5 **Tupa**. Tower
6 **Paina**. Ceremonial circle
7 **Taheta**. Stone basin for rainwater
8 Petroglyph
9 **Umu pae**. Cooking oven
10 **Hare paenga**. House
11 **Hare moa**. Chicken house
12 **Manavai**. Garden enclosure

Cross section of an ahu

Throughout the megalithic phase (**Ahu-Moai**) the **ahu** underwent modification and expansion from a simple rectangular platform, sometimes taking advantage of a rock promontory. Some elements such as the **moai** were used in the new walls during subsequent expansions. After the destruction of the **ahu** and the fall of the **moai**, burial chambers (**avanga**) were built underneath the platform and under the fallen **moai**.

1 **Moai**. Statue
2 **Pukao**. Topknot
3 **Paenga**. Basalt Slab
4 Scoria lintel
5 Early ramp
6 Plaza
7 **Tahua**. Front ramp
8 **Avanga**. Burial chamber (Late Period)
9 **Papa henua**. Bedrock
10 **Poro**. Beach boulder
11 **Puku**. Outcrop
12 Early **ahu**
13 First plaza floor

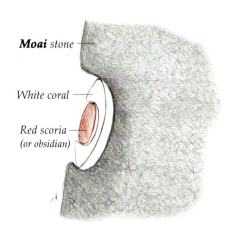

Moai stone
White coral
Red scoria (or obsidian)

Scoria lintel
Basalt slab

WEST COAST
TAHAI CEREMONIAL COMPLEX

AHU KO TE RIKU *Reconstructed by Mulloy, Ayres, and Figueroa between 1968 and 1970, this* **ahu** *has only one* **moai** *on the platform. The* **pukao** *is a replica, and the eyes were made and set in place by an islander around 1990.*

as the construction of walls of polished basalt and lintels of red volcanic scoria, for use as sites for the erection of ever larger and ever more stylized **moai**.

Some of them were capped off by **pukao**, a topknot made of red volcanic scoria, representing hair tied into a bun and dyed with red ochre (**kie'a**) as a symbol of high rank. At times, the last visible stage included fragments of preexisting **moai** from a former stage of that same **ahu**, and in exceptional cases, designs in bas-relief, such as in the **Ahu Nau Nau** at **Anakena**. The perfection of the setting and finishing of blocks of stone of the **Ahu Vinapu** (**Vinapu** 1 or **Tahiri**) shows an extraordinary technical capability, as well as the power reflected in the proportions of **Ahu Tongariki**, with a central platform 45 meters long that at one time supported 15 colossal **moai**, with lateral extensions that made for a total length of 150 meters.

*The stage of megalithic expansion on the island must have begun towards the end of the first millennium of the Christian era. The last **ahu** were constructed around the seventeenth century, which means that in a relatively brief period of time the **Rapanui** society concentrated on the construction of around 300 **ahu** and around 1,000 **moai**.*

*In the beginning, the **ahu** were rather small, low platforms with small **moai** having more naturalistic forms. It also appears that the first **moai** were carved out of other raw materials, such as volcanic scoria, trachyte, or basalt, besides the **Rano Raraku** tuff. As these groups became more powerful, they enlarged the platforms and reused old **moai** to make parts of new walls. In the late phase, a time of destruction of the statues (the **Huri-Moai** phase), the **ahu** were destroyed in part and modified to accommodate collective burials (**avanga**) under the platforms. In some cases, they were covered over with stones to make up what has been called a "semi-pyramidal **ahu**".*

*An interesting type of architecture is termed **Ahu Poe Poe**, due to its boat-like shape, comprised of an elongated rectangular structure pointed and raised at the ends, making it look similar to a boat. Normally they have a chamber running the length of the structure with a series of openings through to the roof. These characteristics make this structure more similar to a funerary construction, to representations of boats made of mud (**miro o'one**), or even to a type of **hare moa** (chicken houses) than to a true **ahu**. Around twelve remain in existence, and are concentrated on the northern coast.*

*An aspect which is interesting to stress is that the **ahu** originally were not used as a repository for the bodies of members of each lineage. In the classical period they were the locations for small cremation sites in the form of small, rectangular cists next to the back wall of the **ahu**. The funeral chambers (**avanga**) were late additions to the **ahu**, constructed under the inclined platform (**tahua**), or even as small chambers made by enclosing the available space beneath fallen **moai** with stone walls. This fundamental change in the manner of disposal of the dead must have been an adaptation to a lack of fuel for cremation. The use of these structures as secondary burial places continued until recent times, insofar as each family recognized its belonging to a given territory.*

AHU VAI URI *(Tahai Ceremonial Complex)*

THE ONLY MOAI OF AHU TAHAI IS SHOWN IN THE FOREGROUND *(Tahai Ceremonial Complex)*

SOUTH COAST
AHU VINAPU

This famous **ahu** is located at the edge of the eastern slope of **Rano Kau**, above the cliff of **Hanga Te Pau**, the site where the seven legendary explorers disembarked.

It is actually two **ahu**, referred to in literature as **Vinapu** I and II. The first one, traditionally called **Ahu Tahiri**, is notable for the exceptional quality of its masonry. Although it is of relatively modest size, the seawall is made from huge polished basalt blocks that were joined using perfectly matching cuts.

The quality of the work, especially the "pillow" shape of the blocks, reminds one of the Inca walls at Cuzco and Sacsayhuaman. However, the date assigned to **Vinapu**, around 1200 A.D., is a couple of centuries older than the Inca structures.

In its current, unrestored state, the **Ahu Tahiri** has five overturned **moai** on the ramp (**tahua**), large **pukao** that were rolled onto the plaza, and funeral chambers built underneath the bodies of the **moai**, where a number of bleached bones had been deposited.

The remains of the village can be seen higher up on the mountain slope, with a few poorly-preserved **hare paenga**. Of interest here are the remains of a house with the same structure as those at **Orongo**, which had been used as a burial place. A complete body was deposited in a fetal position.

An important feature at **Ahu Vinapu** II, larger in size but with a simple seawall, is a red scoria figure located in front of the structure. This sculpture differs in design from the classic **moai**. It is a narrow monolith, with a long, rectangular body and feminine features. Although the head is broken, there is an old graphic reference that ascribes it two heads.

AHU VAIHU
(HANGA TE'E)

*The eight **moai** of this **ahu** remain toppled on the platform. The **pukao** rolled forward, two of them even all the way to the sea. Although the back wall is not high, it is impressive in both length and the quality of the stonework, making it the foremost monument for a vast territory.*

AHU HANGA TETENGA

*This **ahu**, with only two **moai**, was severely altered by destruction in ancient times and, later, by the sheep company. One of these **moai**, 10 meters high, used to be one of the two largest to be raised onto an **ahu**.*

The Moai
Rano Raraku

The **moai**, the symbol of **Rapa Nui**, have become a universal icon. They were a dominant element of the landscape of the island until their destruction between the seventeenth and the early nineteenth centuries. These stylized statues were the embodiment of the spirits of the ancestors of each lineage. The proper names of some of them have even been salvaged from the past.

A total of 838 **moai** have been recorded on the island. Of these, 397 are found in the **Rano Raraku** quarry, 288 are associated with **ahu**, and the rest are scattered around different points of the island, probably having been abandoned en route to some **ahu**. Of the total, 784 were carved out of the lapilli tuff of **Rano Raraku**, 22 out of white trachyte, 18 out of red volcanic scoria, and 10 out of basalt.

The selection of the quarries at **Maunga Eo** (fragrant hill), better known as **Rano Raraku**, was probably due to the fact that the grayish yellow volcanic rock found only here, a type called lapilli tuff, made of compact volcanic ash with incrustations of small pieces of basalt, was a raw material of intermediate workability characteristics between the soft trachyte or volcanic scoria and the extremely hard basalt, accessible for massive construction of statues through the use of simple basalt picks and adzes (**toki**).

The lapilli tuff is found in the southern half of the crater walls, which are higher on this side.

The northern half, which lowers gently in height, is made up of a friable reddish material. The activities of the ancient expert carvers of stone images (**tangata maori anga moai maea**) were focused on the outer wall that looks to the southwest. But work reached the very summit and even over to the opposite edge towards the interior of the crater, on whose slopes more than 40 statues looking towards the lagoon have withstood the ravages of time.

Indeed, one of the remaining "mysteries" in practical terms is to understand why the islanders chose not to simply quarry out the blocks of raw material to haul them off to a more comfortable place to be worked on by the sculptors, and why, instead, these figures were carved out to include practically all of their details, and even the finer details of the face and hands, before the stone was wrested from its niche of origin in the high part of the quarry.

The cutting began on one side while facing the vertical wall or by working downwards where horizontal or even considerably inclined surfaces existed, with the head of the figure located at the top or at the bottom. However, the back was always turned until a keel was cut all along the long axis of the body,

THE LAKE INSIDE RANO RARAKU VOLCANO

in such a manner as to be able to move in this position along the hillside to the bottom of the hill, where a hole had been prepared to allow the figure to be placed standing. In this position, the carving of the back would be finished, and the figure would be in position to "walk" towards its final destination.

This entire operation must have required an enormous amount of skill, and an abundant use of timber and strong vegetal fiber ropes. A series of cylindrical orifices can be observed in one sector of the summit, called **Pu Makari** (page 79). Although they may have been used to install heavy beams and ropes, they are located above a marginal area of the main quarries; hence, their purpose is not entirely clear.

On the hillside are enormous accumulations of leftover material produced by the carving of hundreds of **moai** over a period of several centuries, along with thousands of flakes from the sharpening of the points of the basalt tools. Also, it is still possible to see the marks of picks (**toki**) in the walls of the carved-out niches where the figures were hewn. The tuff would be softer for working if soaked first with abundant water and would then harden again.

The millions of blows from these hand-held picks appear to have come to a standstill all at the same time. Hundreds of **moai** were left in various stages of carving. Although they were abandoned in some cases due to technical problems or fractures, the impression gained on site is that for some reason this enormous work was interrupted abruptly. It would appear that the tools had been left waiting for the return of the workers at any time.

The aesthetics of the classical images that came out of the **Rano Raraku** quarries exhibit a clearly defined pattern whose variations are associated with a stylization. They also increase in size with the passage of time, with exceptional shapes to be noted such as

Rano Raraku volcano

the so-called "**Tukuturi**" (kneeling) **moai** (page 75). The oldest statues have faces with more naturalistic features, trapezoidal or round heads, and are found in the first stages of construction of the **ahu**. In certain cases, it is possible to see them, rescued during the reconstruction of an **ahu** at its stage of maximum splendor, such as **Ahu Tongariki**, or incorporated into the last expansion of a rear wall, such as **Ahu Nau Nau** (page 98). According to a local tradition related to the statue called **Tai Hare Atua**, abandoned on the outer slope of **Rano Raraku**, the origin of the shape has a clearly phallic connotation.

The standard statues of rectangular shape are noteworthy for having heads proportionately larger than the body, with elongated noses in which the flares are delineated with fine spirals, mouths with thin lips and a disdainful expression, and ears with long earlobes, in which at times there are cylindrical earrings. Chins have a pronounced edge, occasionally finishing in a small rectangular beard. The eyes were made to remain closed until the figure was erected on an **ahu**.

The bodies were designed in such a manner as to have a low center of gravity, with a swollen abdomen in the lower third and a concave back. The base was cut off at the lower level of the pelvis, covering the genitals in the front with a loincloth (**hami**). The arms were held tight against a relatively wide body and projected towards the **hami**. The hands are striking with their long fine fingers, thumbs curved upwards. The breasts have nipples modeled as spirals in bas-relief. Under the thick neck a line is used to represent collarbones, and at the center, a cleft marks the upper part of the breastbone. The navel is marked in bas-relief, although due to erosion it is no longer distinguishable in most cases.

In ancient times, probably all of the **moai** that had actually been erected on

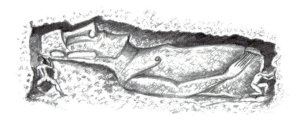 

Carving, Transport, and Installation

In this case, the expert carvers worked by advancing along a vertical wall until completely surrounding the figure, with all of its features. The keel was cut free, and the figure was made to slide down the hillside until it fell into a hole prepared at the base of the slope, where the profile of the back was touched up and the figure was left ready to be transported.

*A **moai** from the quarry inside of **Rano Raraku** crater, attached to the niche along its back, in the process of being cut loose. The volcano's reed-covered lake can be seen in the background.*

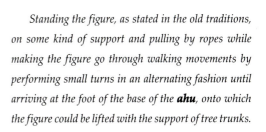

*One alternative involves carrying the **moai** lying face down on a wooden sledge, which was then made to skid across the ground on trunks, and not necessarily on rollers. It was necessary to protect the delicate features of the face and the hands under the belly.*

Noted here are the two most feasible transport alternatives.

*Standing the figure, as stated in the old traditions, on some kind of support and pulling by ropes while making the figure go through walking movements by performing small turns in an alternating fashion until arriving at the foot of the base of the **ahu**, onto which the figure could be lifted with the support of tree trunks.*

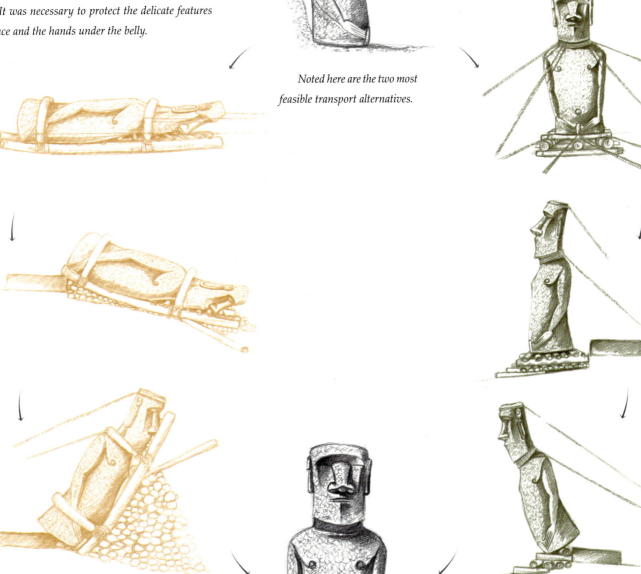

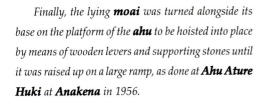

*Finally, the lying **moai** was turned alongside its base on the platform of the **ahu** to be hoisted into place by means of wooden levers and supporting stones until it was raised up on a large ramp, as done at **Ahu Ature Huki** at **Anakena** in 1956.*

*The climactic moment was the opening of the cavities and the setting in place of the coral eyes, which marked the consecration of the statue as the living face and body of an ancestor, the embodiment of its **mana** and its projection to the descendents and their territory for generations.*

UNFINISHED MOAI ON AN OUTER SLOPE OF RANO RARAKU

*an **ahu** were painted with red **kie'a**. Some have incised designs representing tattoos on the neck. The **moai** of **Ahu Nau Nau** at **Anakena** have geometric designs in bas-relief, applied on the back, such as a belt at the height of the hips, designed in the form of an M or a Y, along with spirals on the buttocks. At **Rano Raraku** many of the **moai** have engravings that probably date from a later period, related to the birdman cult, but are also an insignia of rank of the **Ariki**, such as the **reimiro** (carved wood pectoral in crescent form, page 118), old boats and, in one case, of a European ship, which reflects a continuity of the culture and a permanent reference to the "**mana**" of these images.*

*The average height of the **moai** is around 4.5 meters, but the ancient specialists were capable of sculpting and moving two statues measuring ten meters high, which were taken to **Ahu Hanga Tetenga** (page 63) on the southern coast, and **Ahu Te Pito Kura** (page 93) on the northern coast, the area of La Pérouse, around six kilometers away from the quarry.*

*At the main quarry of **Rano Raraku**, there is an image measuring 21.65 meters in length, known as **Te Tokanga** which, although not cut out and released from its niche, would have weighed more than 200 tons, something that is still unthinkable for even the most modern technology. The largest statues were abandoned on the downhill slopes from the quarry, which shows that the **Rapanui** society had, for some reason, embarked on a competition that was finally resolved through total abandonment of megalithism.*

*According to local tradition, the giant measuring more than 20 meters was intended to be taken to **Ahu Vinapu**. Around 164 **moai** were actually taken to different **ahu** distributed all around*

the contour of the island, while some were placed inland. At times they form imposing groups, such as the 15 **moai** at **Ahu Tongariki** (page 88), with individual weights running more than 60 tons, or the group of seven of the normal type **moai** at **Ahu Akivi** (page 106). Also to be noted is the unique specimen represented by the **moai** named **Paro**, with its impressive height of 10 meters, which was additionally topped off by an enormous **pukao** two meters in diameter, at **Ahu Te Pito Kura**.

According to calculations by Prof. William Mulloy, this last **moai** must have required one year for 30 men to carve it out, two months for 90 men to haul it from the quarry, and five months for 90 men to install it on the platform.

The controversial issue of the hauling technique for these enormous, heavy statues, which at the same time had fine features carved on a fragile surface, has still not been solved satisfactorily. However, upon ruling out several fantastic or ridiculous conjectures, there are a number of serious hypotheses and experiments that have been able to demonstrate that such transport was feasible with the human resources and materials that the ancient islanders had at hand.

According to local tradition, the **moai** walked. Several roads leading out from the volcano were used to transport the statues (**Ko te Ara O Te Moai**). Still visible is the road that followed along the southern coast, where several statues toppled face down can still be found.

The ephemeral power of man and the immortal strength of the rock. In a vertically arranged niche, the lifeless body of a giant stands out above all those located behind. Jutting out at the base are the heads of those that were left in walking position.

EARLY MOAI	MOAI "HOA HAKA NANA IA"	MOAI AHU HURI A URENGA	MOAI AHU ATURE HUKI	MOAI AHU KO TE RIKU
0.60 - 1.4 MTS.	2.5 MTS.	3 MTS.	3.5 MTS.	4.5 - 5 MTS.
Trapezoidal heads. More naturalistic features. Group visible behind **Ahu Tongariki**.	Made of basalt. Once located at the **Orongo** Ceremonial Village.	Faces the winter solstice. Has 4 hands.	Located at **Anakena**. The first to be returned to a standing position in 1956.	Located at **Tahai**, has been restored.

PAINTED MOAI

The **moai** were originally engraved and painted, most likely in several colors, in work carried out at different times and for different purposes, whether while still in the quarry, on an **ahu**, or even after having been abandoned.

A **moai** at **Rano Raraku** has tattooing on its neck, opposing chevron marks radiating from a center which still show traces of red pigment. The same **moai** bears an image of **Make Make** carved in bas-relief on its left shoulder, a detail that indicates a reuse or symbolic overlay on the central motif of the preceding period.

MOAI AHU	MOAI "PARO"	MOAI "TE TOKANGA"
TONGARIKI	AHU TE PITO KURA	THE GIANT
6 - 8 MTS.	10 MTS.	21.65 MTS.

*15 restored **moai**, at the largest **ahu**.*   *The largest to be erected.*   *A **moai** from the **Rano Raraku** quarry. Never left the quarry.*

THE TOKI

*Whether rough-hewn picks or polished adzes made of the hardest basalt with the finest grain, this was the tool used to carve the **moai**, canoes, and wooden statues. This exceptional 37.5 cm piece is preserved at the Fonck Museum in Viña del Mar (right).*

OUTER QUARRY OF RANO RARAKU

MOAI TUKUTURI. THE ONLY MOAI ON ITS KNEES

A MOAI FROM THE OUTER QUARRY, WITH A EUROPEAN SHIP CARVED ON ITS CHEST

*It has been proven that it is feasible to make a 3-meter-high **moai** walk by rocking it from side to side while alternately pulling forward on each side of the base. The larger **moai** must have been transported while lying down with the aid of thick ropes and protective structures like a wooden sledge. Hoisting it onto the platform must have been the most difficult and complex task, especially when the statues were to be placed very close to each other on an elevated platform without the aid of foundations, reinforcing bars or pulleys.*

An extreme example would involve the lifting of a cylinder of volcanic scoria that may have weighed more than 10 tons, more than ten meters into the air to finally balance it on top of a small surface. Obviously, the engineering behind all of these feats is absolutely astounding, leaps and bounds beyond any other megalithic expression anywhere else in Polynesia.

Of the 164 **moai** erected on an **ahu**, 58 had volcanic scoria cylinders, or **pukao**, placed on top of their heads. These **pukao** were made in the quarry of **Puna Pau**, a small crater located across from **Hanga Roa**.

Thirty-one **pukao** were ultimately abandoned either in the quarry or while being transported out of it. The dimensions of these cylinders were between 1 and 2 meters high by 2 to 3 meters in diameter, with weights running between 9 and 20 tons.

Of course, this involved more than a technical problem alone. What was of most importance for a society like that of **Rapa Nui** was the ideology. The **moai** were intended to embody the living spirit of an ancestor. Until reaching the erection stage on a particular **ahu**, they were nothing more than empty statues. In 1978, the reconstruction of **Ahu Nau Nau** at **Anakena** unearthed the first eye ever to be found, which was made of coral with a red volcanic scoria pupil, which was the image of the living face (**aringa ora**) of an ancestor, and the vehicle for the projection of **mana**. After centuries of destruction and abandonment, the gaze of the **moai** had at last made itself known again.

From their position on an **ahu**, whether looking towards the center of the island from the coast or located farther inland, the **moai** spread this power like a protective cloak over a lineage and its members' territory.

The level achieved by the **Rapanui** Megalithic Culture resulted from a combination of many factors, where competition intensified by enviromental restrictions was expressed precisely in the construction of even larger **ahu** and **moai**. The increasing population number could not be reduced to sustainable levels, so the existing groups underwent divisions and mergers to assure their own survival. Competition between the most powerful groups was inevitable in an environment deteriorated by overexploitation and subject to periodic natural catastrophes. The insistence on and perseverance of megalithism, although ultimately a blind alley, maintained for a while the social cohesion, stability, and order among the groups that were most capable of assuring their access to resources for subsistence.

With the absence of ocean-going craft that could relieve a demographic situation exerting pressure on an insufficient food supply, the **mana** of the ancestors was unable to sustain the society forever. This continued until the entire social, religious, political, and economic system went into crisis. This, besides bringing about the definitive abandonment of megalithism, required a remarkable effort of adaptation to generate new forms of expression throughout all of the culture.

Highest point of Rano Raraku

RANO RARAKU'S LAGOON AND ITS INTERIOR QUARRY

*On the highest point of **Rano Raruku**, called **Pu Makari**, a number of artificial orifices are associated with the installation of trunks and ropes. However, because of their location they do not seem to be related to the sliding of the **moai**, but to an ancient game called **ma'ari**, which consisted of going up and down the volcano cliff with the use of ropes, as in a cableway.*

AHU TONGARIKI

Ahu Tongariki is located next to **Hanga Nui** (the large bay) at the eastern end of the southern coast, on the way to the edge of the **Poike** cliff.

This was the most impressive megalithic monument of the classic period, with a central platform nearly 100 meters long that once supported 15 **moai** with their respective **pukao**.

The statues vary from 5.6 to 8.7 meters tall and weigh an average of 40 tons. The largest statue, with its enormous **pukao** on its head, reached some 14 meters above the level of the plaza.

Like all of the **ahu** on the island, **Tongariki** was intentionally destroyed in the days of the civil wars. All the **moai** were thrown forward except for one whose broken base was in place until 1960. The crack on the body could follow a natural grain of the rock. Interestingly, it has been suggested that earthquakes may have played a role in the fall of the **moai**.

On May 20, 1960, when an earthquake devastated the south of Chile, a gigantic westward-bound wave struck the eastern coast of the island.

It is estimated that the wave reached some 10 meters in height and struck with enough force to lift the **moai**, giant polished basalt blocks of the seawall,

VIEW OF AHU TONGARIKI FROM THE HIGHEST POINT OF RANO RARAKU

*Tongariki. Seen in a silhouette view on the right is the lone **moai** locally called the "travelling **moai**" because it was taken to the Osaka Trade Fair in Japan. In 1986, it "walked" once again, made to do so upon being pulled by ropes in an experiment carried out by a Czechoslovakian engineer invited by Thor Heyerdahl.*

*In front of the impressive **Ahu Tongariki**, at the edge of today's road, there are lava platforms with beautiful engravings and bas-relief carvings depicting fish, turtles, vulvas, **make make**, birdmen, and a series of cupules. Its name, **Papa Tataku Poki**, refers to counting (**tataku**) the number of children (**poki**) of the local tribe (**Hotu Iti**) killed by their enemies from **Hanga Roa** (**Tu'u** tribe).*

MAKE MAKE IN BAS-RELIEF

ENGRAVED TUNA

*A view of the 15 **moai** of **Ahu Tongariki** and of the **Poike** cliffs, and **Motu Marotiri**.*

and thousands of cubic meters of rock and fill from the platform, and scattered them over an area of four hectares. Some of the **moai** were deposited more than 100 meters from their original position.

Starting in 1992 and for the following four years, a team from the University of Chile sponsored by a Japanese crane company rebuilt the impressive monument, which is a landmark both in **Rapa Nui** history and on the island's landscape of today.

After the intentional toppling of the **moai** on the platform and until their final destruction by the tidal wave, the monument became a large ossuary, with large funeral chambers underneath the platform and the plaza.

Especially important among the pieces that were recovered is a group of small **moai** with more natural shapes, permitting the recognition of the older style. These **moai** must have belonged to the early phases of the **ahu**, and were incorporated into the walls or the fill during the successive building stages. Now grouped behind the wall these **moai** display archaic forms with their trapezoid-shaped heads, short ears, and arms crossed over the stomach.

The last **moai**, with the stylization characteristic of the most advanced stage, remained lying down on the plaza in front of the **ahu**. The fact that its eyes, unlike the others, were not open indicates that it was never placed on the platform, so it never became the embodiment of an ancestor's **mana**.

Partial View of Tongariki

Of the 164 **moai** erected on an **ahu**, 58 had volcanic scoria cylinders, or **pukao**, placed on top of their heads. These **pukao** were made in the quarry of **Puna Pau**, a small crater located across from **Hanga Roa**. Thirty-one **pukao** were ultimately abandoned, either in the quarry or while being transported out of it. The dimensions of these cylinders were between 1 and 2 meters high by 2 to 3 meters in diameter, with weights running between 9 and 20 tons. A cavity at the base allowed it to fit onto the narrow top of the statue and balance in such a way as to jut out over the eyes.

Twilight with moon

POIKE
PENINSULA

AERIAL VIEW OF POIKE PENINSULA

This was the first portion of **Rapa Nui** Island to emerge from the sea as a result of volcanic eruptions approximately 3 million years ago.

POIKE DITCH

Poike Ditch, traditionally known as *"Ko Te Umu O Te Hanau E'epe"* (The Curanto of the **Hanau E'epe**), is another of the island's "mysteries." The legend refers to the place of the last battle between the **Hanau E'epe** and the **Hanau Momoko**. The former had taken refuge on the **Poike** Peninsula, protected by a ditch at the base of the hill, to which they set fire. The **Hanau Momoko** took them by surprise and killed nearly everyone in the ditch. However, archaeological excavations revealed that the ditch was not for defensive purposes, but a series of 20 to 30 ditches some five meters apart that may have been dedicated to agriculture.

*A monumental sculpture in **Poike** known as **Vai A Heva**, whose mouth is a natural cavity for the collection of rainwater (the water of **Heva**).*

ANA O KEKE CAVE
The Legend of the Neru

*One of the most curious legends refers to the custom of isolating and confining young virgins (**neru**) in caves to whiten their skin. The chosen sites were caves in the inaccessible cliffs on the eastern **Poike** peninsula. The entrance to the cave of the **neru** called **Ana O Keke** can be reached from the north cliff of **Poike** through a small opening that leads to a smooth-walled lava pipe. In the section of this pipe nearest its entrance a row of unique, fine engravings can be seen, amongst which is a **toki** mounted on a haft, a phytomorphic figure and, especially noteworthy, a figure which combines human and geometric elements. The narrow cave follows a winding course, with some areas flooded and others where the tunnel is no more than 40 cm high. The tunnel is approximately 380 meters deep.*

*View looking towards a small sea squall from the top of **Pua Katiki**, elevation 370 meters, the highest peak of the **Poike** peninsula and the second highest on the island.*

THE POIKE PENINSULA IS USED FOR LIVESTOCK GRAZING

NORTH COAST

*View of **Poike**'s north side. In the foreground the severely eroded **Maunga Parehe**, followed by **Maunga Tea Tea** and **Maunga Vai A Heva**, finishing with the highest, **Maunga Pua Katiki**, with a small forest in the inner part of the crater.*

AHU TE PITO KURA

Ahu Te Pito Kura *located on the north coast. It has a rather small wall which, until the early nineteenth century, supported the heavy **Moai Te Paro**, the largest ever erected anywhere on the island, measuring 10 meters high without counting the additional 2 meters of the **pukao** on the top. It was the last **moai** to be overturned.*

*This semi-spheric beach boulder, which was originally found on one of the wings of **Ahu Te Pito Kura**, is now called **Te Pito O Te Henua** (The Navel of the World) and has become a post-modern cult object, where tourists come to fill themselves with its "**mana**."*

OVAHE

*The small **Ovahe** Bay has as a backdrop the steep cliff of loose red volcanic scoria, which forms the eastern flank of **Maunga Puha Roa**.*

ANAKENA

*According to tradition, the legendary King **Hotu Matua** arrived at this small bay. The present name **Anakena** actually refers to a small cave used by the migratory bird named **kena** (Sula dactylatra), located above a ravine whose water in old times reached the beach, the early **Hanga Mori A One** (Bay of the Shining Sand).*

*Six-centimeter-long bone harpoon found at **Anakena**, dated between 1100-1200 AD. Unique among the findings made to date, it shows ties with the Marquesas Islands at a much later date than the first Polynesian contact.*

AHU NAU NAU
ANAKENA

*Restored in 1978 by the islander archaeologist Sergio Rapu, this **ahu** has noteworthy architectural details and unique decoration, with beautiful figures worked in bas-relief on certain blocks of the seawall.*

*All of the **moai** wore elaborate **pukao**, and the platform included two ramps separated by a lintel composed of basalt slabs with inlaid blocks of volcanic scoria. The boulders of the upper ramp were selected to produce a pavement white in color as a result of calcareous deposits.*

*The most important finding was that of an almost complete eye (page 56), made of coral, with a red volcanic scoria disc to represent the iris, inlaid in a circular cavity in the coral. For the first time after several centuries, the **moai** were able to display the living face (**aringa ora**) of the ancestors they were to represent.*

One of the moai of Ahu Nau Nau at Anakena, with a flat conical-shaped Pukao

This view of **Anakena** shows from left to right the base of **Maunga Hau Epa**, a truncated conical hill with a curious notch, a kind of artificial terrace located around the top whose purpose is unknown. Further to the right there can be seen **Ahu Ature Huki** and, nearby, **Ahu Nau Nau**. At the western end of the beach on a rocky promontory is **Ahu Iho Arero**, a simple platform without **moai** but with interesting petroglyphs on some of the blocks of the seaward wall.

The seven **moai** of **Ahu Nau Nau** in **Anakena** had to be special, since they represented the ancestors of the **Ariki Henua** (spiritual leader). In fact, details of the **hami** and spirals representing tattoos on the buttocks are shown on their backs. The statues are not large in size, but they all have red scoria **pukao** on their heads. The architecture of the **Ahu** itself, in its final extension, shows a combination of forms and a selection of different colored stones: white on the upper platform pavement, red on the scoria lintel, and black in the polished basalt blocks. The head of a **moai** from a previous stage can be seen in this section of the seawall.

PAGES 100-101.
AHU NAU NAU AT NIGHT

AHU ATURE HUKI
ANAKENA

AHU ATURE HUKI

*During the famous 1955-56 Norwegian expedition, at a time when no **moai** had been left standing on the entire island as they had been toppled during the eighteenth and nineteenth centuries, it was decided, at the request of Thor Heyerdahl, to erect the massive **moai** of **Ahu Ature Huki** right next to the expedition's campsite. The job was directed by Mayor Pedro Atán, and it took a group of 12 islanders 18 days to raise the four-ton, 3.5-meter-high statue, aided by long trunks used as levers while leaning it on stones piled to form a large ramp.*

AHU ATURE HUKI (*left*), AHU NAU NAU (*right*)

INLAND RAPA NUI

INTERIOR LANDSCAPE

THE SOUTHERN VIEW FROM MAUNGA TEREVAKA'S SLOPES

Maunga Terevaka

Maunga Terevaka was the last landform to emerge from the ocean from volcanic eruptions taking place around 250,000 years ago. Most of the island rain, which must have been even greater when the slopes were covered with forest, falls on the flat grassy uplands of this volcano. The totora-blanketed **Rano Aroi** crater lies near the summit.

Rano Aroi crater

*Small lagoon formed by rainfall close to the peak of **Maunga Terevaka***

*Trails in the upland portion of **Maunga Terevaka**.*

AHU AKIVI

Ahu Akivi was the first **ahu** whose restoration, by Mulloy and Figueroa in 1960, was systematic. It is aligned on an equinoctial north-south axis in such a way that the backs of the **moai** face the rising sun. They appear to gaze towards the sea, but actually they looked towards an inland area, aligned with the small **Ahu Vai Teka**. The fact that **Akivi** has seven **moai** has led to the idea that they represented the seven explorers of the legend of **Hotu Matu'a**.

At the time of restoration and to decorate the surface of the platform, river stones that had been utilized for ballast on a shipwrecked Italian vessel were used.

At the back of the platform there are a number of small rectangular chambers framed by vertical slabs of stone. They were used in ancient times as crematories.

ANA TE PAHU
CAVE

*In a vast area known as **Roiho**, marked by traces of the island's most recent volcanic activity between 6 and 10 thousand years ago, the capricious movement of incandescent lava formed a large number of caves, many of which were used as temporary shelters (**ana kionga**) and adapted as **manavai** for growing a variety of plants. One of the most interesting and accessible caves, **Ana Te Pahu**, can be found on the road between **Ahu Akivi** and **Ahu Tepeu**. Surface magma flowing from **Maunga Hiva Hiva** near **Ahu Akivi** towards the sea swept away all the trees. Interesting samples from these trees' imprints still remain, especially in the cliff overlooking the sea, but even at the entrance to the main chamber of **Te Pahu**. Like most of the caverns, it was modified to be used as a shelter, and the lush growth of a variety of edible species flourishes in its open areas. To this day, one may see native banana and **taro**, along with avocado, grapes, and other introduced species.*

Archaeoastronomy

Knowledge of the movements of the stars, their systematic observation, and the changes in the seasons; the phases of the moon and the establishment of a calendar; the occurrence of phenomena such as eclipses and comets and their magical relations with the lives of men and nature and especially with navigation, ceremonies, and omens; all this formed part of the heritage of ancient **Rapa Nui**.

The Polynesian navigators that colonized **Rapa Nui** possessed quite complete astronomical knowledge, which they put to use in this new land particularly in controlling food production. The subtropical location of the island gives rise to climatic variations throughout the year that have an influence on planting and, additionally, mark seasonal patterns in the times of appearance of birds and fish. The seasons of the year are of different duration, starting with **Tonga Nui**, from late June through August; followed by **Hora Iti**, which lasts until mid October; then **Hora Nui**, extending until March, the period in which most of the festivals were celebrated; and **Tonga Iti**, between April and May, the rainiest season and a time of strong northeasterly winds.

On **Rapa Nui**, the scientific knowledge of the progression of the seasons was accompanied by rites and ceremonies, headed up by the **Ariki**, to make way for the start of planting and harvesting. A twelve-month calendar was defined by the cycles of the moon (**mahina**), starting with each new moon (**ohiro**). The year began with the appearance of the Pleiades (**Matariki**) following the winter solstice. In the last stage of **Rapanui** prehistory, each year bore the name of the victorious **tangata manu**. The phases of the moon, and especially the new moon (**ohiro**) and full moon (**omotohi**) were of great importance for determining the right time for fishing, certain plantings, festivals, and ceremonies.

Knowledge, the domain of experts, helped maintain the prestige of the aristocracy. In this aspect, the old **Rapanui** society included common elements of universal Neolithic cultures whose material works had astronomical significance, such as Stonehenge in England and the Mayan Caracol structure at Chichen Itza in Mexico.

The ideological domain was functional to a stratified society that had to be capable of maintaining a strict social and political order relying for sustenance on a small area endowed with limited resources. Thus the belief in the positive or negative influence of certain stars at special times (**Matamea, Tautoru, Pau**), the possibility of imposing taboos (**tapu**), and propitiation by means of ceremonies under the aegis of the astronomer priests must have been a part of daily life.

The traditions tell of the importance of the sun (**ra'a**), the moon (**mahina**), some planets (**matamea** = Mars), and stars (**Tautoru** = Orion's belt; **Matariki** = Pleiades; **Te Pou** = Sirius; **Nga Vaka** = Alpha and Beta Centauri; **Rei A Tanga** = Antares; **Hetu'u Ahi Ahi** = Venus, the Evening Star); as well as the existence of schools for apprentices and observatories (**Ana U'i Hetu'u**, near **Tahai**). Also to be noted are a number of petroglyphs with astronomical motifs (**Papa U'i Hetu'u** at **Poike** and **Papa Mahina**, near **Ahu Ra'ai**) and the possible use of certain towers (**tupa**) as astronomical observatories.

However, the most spectacular evidence is provided by the **ahu** themselves, some of which were precisely oriented to mark the solstices and the equinoxes.

*According to modern astronomical data, towards the end of the first millennium of the Christian Era, the time when the **Rapanui** megalithic culture began its development in earnest (the **Ahu-Moai** phase), the islanders would have been able to witness an extraordinary number of solar eclipses (**he kai i te ra'a**) and comets (**hetu'u ave**). There are many sites whose names are tied to the subject of astronomy.*

*According to recent investigation by the astronomer William Liller, around 20 **ahu** were intentionally placed in astronomically significant locations to have the **moai** directly facing sunrise or sunset at the times of solstices or equinoxes.*

In general, the inland **ahu** with astronomical orientation are linked with the solstices, especially the winter solstice, while the astronomically oriented ahu along the coast are placed with equinoctial north-south orientation in such a manner as to have the **moai** looking straight east or west, like the famous **Ahu Akivi**. This could be explained by the fact that the **moai** along the coast were placed in relation to precise positions from the sea, while those located inland had agricultural significance, particularly at the winter solstice, when there would be the least amount of solar radiation and the day was the shortest, at the onset of winter.

The most notable astronomical monument is **Ahu Huri A Urenga**, which faces the sun as it rises behind **Poike** at the winter solstice, in line with **Maunga Mataengo**. Beside the plaza there are some circular cavities that would also have astronomical significance.

At **Vinapu**, **Ahu Tahiri** marks the equinoxes, and **Ahu Vinapu** 2, the summer solstice. **Ahu Ra'ai** and **Tongariki** also mark the summer solstice. From **Orongo**, the winter solstice can be observed exactly in line with **Pua Katiki**, which could give this place a special connotation as the place selected for holding the **tangata manu** ceremony. Some circular cavities located alongside a small **ahu** near the first houses do not appear to have any astronomical significance, although it has been said that the shadow cast by a rod placed in one of these holes may mark the seasons of the year, the kind of knowledge which must have been used for the timely preparation of the ceremony.

Ideology

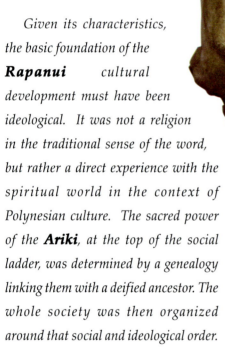

Given its characteristics, the basic foundation of the **Rapanui** cultural development must have been ideological. It was not a religion in the traditional sense of the word, but rather a direct experience with the spiritual world in the context of Polynesian culture. The sacred power of the **Ariki**, at the top of the social ladder, was determined by a genealogy linking them with a deified ancestor. The whole society was then organized around that social and ideological order.

The great "gods" of the Polynesian pantheon (**Tane, Tangaroa, Rongo, Oro**) do not appear on **Rapa Nui**, except for a reference to **Tangaroa** in the genealogy of **Ariki Hotu A Matu'a** and in a legend relating his arrival on the island in the shape of a seal, to be nearly devoured by a group of islanders on the northern coast.

In any case, understanding **Rapa Nui** as a phenomenon means grasping the importance of that other dimension by means of a basic concept: the spiritual power, the **mana**, and the fact that all supernatural beings have an earthly and human origin.

Mana can be inherited by right, as in the case of the **Ariki**, or it may be displayed through a special talent, such as being a good fisherman. It may be transmitted to other people or things, or they may be "contaminated" by it, either positively or negatively. It can also be found in nature's elements. It is concentrated particularly in the head, but its power may be preserved in the bones. This explains the use of human skulls, sometimes with designs carved on the forehead, placed inside the **hare moa** (chicken houses) to increase hens' fertility. The origin of the tradition of making fishhooks from human bones lies in using the bones of a fisherman who had evidenced great talent for fishing during his life. Many natural objects, even rocks, could by their very nature embody **mana**, or could obtain it through consecration by individuals with power and through the graphic application of the fertility symbol (**komari**). The **mana** these objects acquired was used to influence food production, agriculture, fishing, and hens, as well as for the protection of homes or places. Just as one may inherit or acquire **mana**, one can also lose it or be a victim of it, either due to the action of a more powerful **mana** or through a serious violation of some precept (**tapu**). The greatest expression of this phenomenon, with all its connotations, can be seen in the **moai** themselves. They were moved

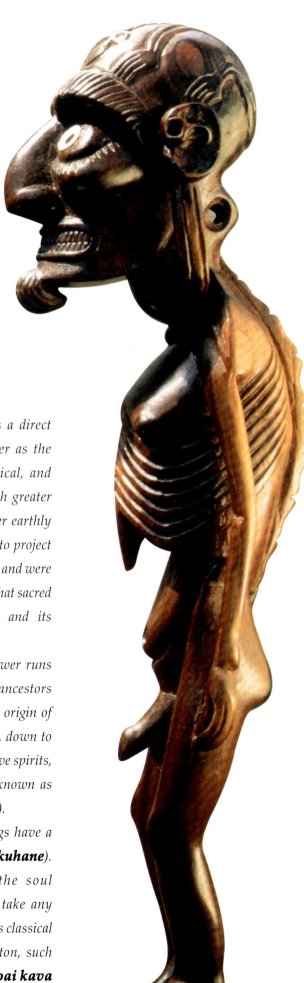

thanks to the **mana** (not as a direct supernatural force, but rather as the expression of a social, political, and religious order that acted with greater coercive power than any other earthly force), then were consecrated to project that power through their gaze, and were finally destroyed to eliminate that sacred connection between a tribe and its ancestral lands.

The expression of this power runs the gamut from the deified ancestors (**atua**), who may become the origin of all things, including mankind, down to the most basic level of protective spirits, in the wide range of spirits known as **aku aku** (**varua** in Tahitian).

In principle, human beings have a body (**hakari**) and a soul (**kuhane**). According to tradition, the soul survives the body and may take any form, human or animal, but its classical expression is that of a skeleton, such as that represented by the **moai kava kava**.

In fact, one of the best known legends refers to **Ariki Tu'u Ko Ihu**, who saw two **aku aku**, called **Hitirau** and **Nuku Te Mango**, sleeping near **Puna Pau**. When he arrived home in the village of **Ahu Tepeu**, he carved their cadaverous images in wood, establishing the model for the moai with protruding ribs (**kava kava**) in order to dominate them. The spirits then appeared before him as young mortals.

Spirits appear even in the least known episodes of the legendary origin of the **Rapanui** people. Even before the astral voyage of **Haumaka**'s spirit, in the manuscript containing the traditions of **Pua Ara Hoa**, reference is made to **Ariki Taana**, the grandfather of **Hotu A Matu'a**, who sent his three sons to the island, where they were turned into **Motu Kao Kao, Motu Iti**, and **Motu Nui** by an evil spirit. Spirits appear in every episode of the legend, playing the role of guides or protective guardians, as masters of some art (tattooing,

MOAI KAVA KAVA

fishhook making), or as vengeful or evil beings. Information has also been recorded on the actions of priests or shamans called **tumu ivi atu'a**, who were able to ward off and dominate negative spirits.

Ariki Hotu A Matu'a's protective spirits, known as **Kuihi** and **Kuaha**, appear at different times. They returned to **Hiva** in search of the broken statue of **Oto Uta**. They protected him during the conflict with **Oroi** and they were at his side at the moment of his death. His spirit then appears as a mouse, while the most powerful **mana** is preserved in his skull.

At the beginning of the century, English researcher Katherine Routledge discovered references to some 90 **aku aku** by name, associated with specific territories all over the island. **Mataveri Otai** was identified as one of the two **aku aku** in the territory of the same name at the foot of **Rano Kau**. Today, very few are familiar with some of these traditions, but the belief in a spirit world of ancestors and their territories lives on.

At a more earthly level, spirits could assume the shape of objects or people, have children with humans, and even die and be reincarnated under the power of a more predominant being.

Tapu, or that which is taboo, is an expression of the supernatural power, **mana**. A specific territory was **tapu** for anybody not directly associated with it, be they living beings or spirits. Individuals with power (**mana**) could alter people and inanimate objects, making them **tapu**.

By the end of **Rapa Nui**'s prehistory, **Make Make** was widely recognized as a "deity", but with rather vague attributes. Clearly associated with the **tangata manu** ceremony, according to tradition, his image carved in bas-relief (mainly a mask surrounding the eyes) seems to represent the embodiment of his spirit in a skull.

Make Make and **Haua**, another spirit only mentioned as a companion, were in charge of bringing the birds from **Motu Motiro Hiva** (Salas and Gómez Island) to the **motu** facing **Rano Kau**. The figure of **Make Make** appeared for the first time as a universal cult and a new political order throughout the island, while the sacred **Ariki Henua** maintained his inherited privileges, safe in the untouchable lands of **Anakena**.

MOAI KAVA KAVA   MAKE MAKE

Wood and Rock Carvings

In ancient times craftsmen carved a variety of ceremonial objects, symbols of aristocratic rank, or images of spirits, despite the scarcity of wood (**miro**) as a raw material.

Toromiro, whose red color made it especially sacred, was among the types of wood most valued for their quality.

In fact, the few **toromiro** objects preserved in museums are priceless, particularly the tablets carved with **rongo rongo** scripts. Besides the variety of foreign woods introduced on the island, such as the **miro tahiti**, the most highly prized wood today is the **mako'i**, a very rare species.

The primary tool used by expert carvers, a job reserved for men, was the **toki**, or **kautoki**. In ancient times, the adze blade of polished stone (fine-grained basalt) was tied at an angle to a hardwood handle with a fine cord made of plant fibers. After rough-hewing the basic form, the artisan

Nowadays, master wood sculptors do not use stone **toki** tools for their work, employing instead sharp steel knives that allow carvings to be made faster, while maintaining the same quality.

MOAI TANGATA   MOAI TANGATA   MOAI VI'E

*used small chisels, knives, and scrapers of basalt or obsidian to carve the details. Obsidian made it easy to craft a variety of easily replaceable cutting instruments, including small drills. Finally, the surface was finished with coral files, sanding tools made from the rough surface of obsidian blocks (**here here**), and was polished to a perfect porcelain finish with **pure** shells.*

*Among the most interesting figures are images of male spirits (**moai tangata** and **kava kava**), female spirits (**moai vi'e** and **pa'a pa'a**), and animal spirits (**moko miro**, a wooden lizard with human features; **manu uru**, a bird; **patuki**, a fish; **honu**, a turtle). The **reimiro**, a crescent-shaped chest ornament, was the distinctive sign of the **Ariki**. There were two types of double-bladed paddles. The largest of these, the **ao**, was the symbol of power, while the smallest, the **rapa**, was used in certain ceremonial dances along with both long (**ua**) and short (**paoa**) war clubs. Among the ceremonial objects is the **tahonga**, apparently the image of an egg, associated with rituals like the puberty initiation ceremony (**poki manu**).*

There is also a variety of special or unique figures, such as images of human hands, rooster heads, figures combining human and animal features, two-headed beings, or women with artificially elongated genitals.

As a result of contact with the Western world, the exchange of ancient sacred objects for fabrics or knives

gradually gave way to the production of objects without **mana**, crafted artlessly in larger sizes suitable for being transported by passing ships. On the other hand, the penetrating influence of the Church replaced ancient ideologies, which can be seen in the remarkable religious images in the **Hanga Roa** church.

In recent years, the market has turned towards a more refined production of traditional objects with greater commercial value. The most expert craftsmen take these models from museum catalogues or specialized publications, and from those requested by tourists while visiting the island. This new demand has not only given birth to a variety of handicrafts sold at the airport, but has also stimulated the revival of the innate talents of the more contemporary carvers, who have displayed their works in art exhibits abroad.

The classic **Rano Raraku moai** is produced on a large scale, having become a truly universal icon, as is the **Hoa Haka Nana Ia moai**. Both are made in wood and stone.

Especially noteworthy among the new pieces are traditional art motifs derived from **rongo rongo** script or petroglyphs. They are used on objects like fruit bowls, necklaces, bracelets, canes, chess sets, etc. Traditional designs are also recreated on large blocks of stone, wood, or coral, and even on silver and gold jewelry. In general, there is a search for new and more highly refined aesthetic expressions, motivated by a public that is more sensitive to **Rapanui** quality and aesthetics.

Modern Reproductions

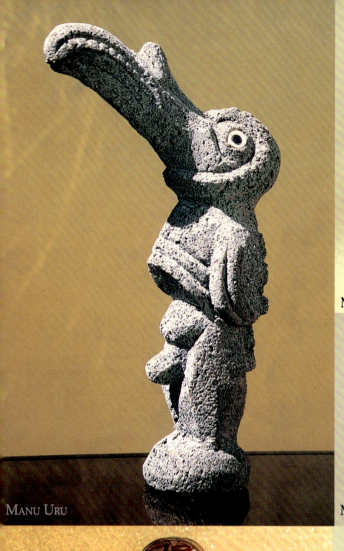

Manu Uru

Moko *(front)*

Moko *(back)*

Moai Kava Kava

Reimiro

Honu

of Classical Figures

Tahonga

Tangata Manu

Classical Moai

Moai Hoa Haka Nana Ia

RONGO RONGO

One of the most notable expressions of the uniqueness of the **Rapanui** culture is its hieroglyphic writing known as **rongo rongo**.

Its origin is still unknown, as there is nothing similar to it in Polynesia or other parts of the world. One of the greatest controversies is over when and how it appeared on the island, since the first European to identify a "talking board" (**Kohau Rongo Rongo**) was Missionary Eugene Eyraud in 1864, who provided very little information. The tablets, made of **toromiro** wood, are engraved with elaborate, stylized designs. Other than being highly elaborated they give no hint as to their development.

The lack of information has caused some to suggest that this writing evolved as a result of contact with Europe, after the "signing" of the document ceding the island to King Charles III of Spain during the expedition led by Felipe González y Aedo in 1770. Some of the chiefs used ink to etch some designs evoking **rongo rongo** symbols, but in a very rough style, on a sheet of paper bearing a text unintelligible to the islanders.

It is highly unlikely that mid-19th century islanders would have been able to develop **rongo rongo** writing. The legend of **Hotu Matu'a** itself, taken from the **Pua Ara Hoa** manuscript, mentions the writing of the names of the places visited by **Mako'i**, the youngest of the seven explorers sent to find the locations described in **Haumaka**'s dream, on a piece of vegetal fiber.

In any case, the writing was only for specialists (**Tangata Maori Rongo Rongo**), priests related to the highest aristocracy. One of the few pieces of information conserved in **Rapanui** tradition is that the initiates had to demonstrate their knowledge periodically by reciting the boards' texts in front of the **Ariki Henua**.

These specialists in ancient traditions and rituals, entrusted with reciting the genealogies, teaching legends, and directing songs and rituals, were also found on the Marquesas Islands and on Mangareva, the closest points which could have had an influence on the **Rapanui** culture. In fact there were specialists called **Tahuna O'ono** and **Taura Rongo Rongo**. On the Tuamotu Islands, the word **rongo** refers to the great deeds of a hero as retold by a specialist.

Since Brother Eyraud's discovery, some 25 wooden tablets engraved with hieroglyphs have been discovered, all of which are preserved in various museums and collections around the world, none on **Rapa Nui**.

Rongo Rongo tablet

*The symbols are markedly conventional. Among them are figures of men, birds, birdmen, two-headed birds, vulvas, hands, feet, fish, turtles, crabs, octopuses, different kinds of plants, utensils, obsidian projectiles, canoes, chest ornaments (**reimiro**), suns, moons, stars, and a variety of geometric designs.*

A symbol possibly representing the breadfruit tree, which was never introduced onto the island, would indicate that the writing originated in a tropical region, the homeland of the Polynesian colonizers.

All together, around 150 basic symbols made up 1500 to 2000 different compositions. A highly relevant feature of the anthropomorphic symbols is the use of body positions, undoubtedly originating from a pantomime language, and the hand symbols, from sign language. Both expressions are characteristic of various Polynesian cultures. However, similar elements can be observed in the ritual dances and theater of Indonesia, China, and Japan.

These signs and compositions do not make up a grammatical structure in the strict sense of the word. They are rather ideograms with various meanings expressed in a telegraphic way, only decipherable by initiates familiar with the codes.

*Some symbols can be interpreted by themselves, such as the image of the creator god **Make Make** and the numerous shapes that represent recognizable elements. But as yet, attempts to understand their true meaning have been futile.*

With the disappearance of the wise men around the mid-1800's due to slave expeditions and epidemics that nearly exterminated the population, the possibility of deciphering the tablets is minimal, despite all efforts to date.

The symbols were engraved on horizontal, slightly concave bands using sharpened sharks' teeth or obsidian flakes. Reading began on the bottom line, and went from left to right. When reaching the end of the line, the reader turned the tablet upside down and continued on the next line up, which was engraved upside down with respect to the previous line. This unusual system of writing is known as "bustrofedon", after the furrow made when plowing with oxen.

*According to the most reliable research, the tablets recorded mainly atemporal religious motifs, and political events or genealogies were rare. Historical events were recorded using another system of writing called **ta'u**. Some engravings referred to procreation and fertility, particularly those on one of the boards preserved at the Natural History Museum in Santiago.*

Rock Art

When considering all of the archaeological remains on the island, rock art might seem less important than the megalithic expressions, such as the **ahu** and the **moai**.

Nevertheless, rock art surpasses all other expressions of this type anywhere else in Polynesia in both quantity and quality.

By combining aesthetics with complex themes, rock carvings and paintings provide insight into the society's myths, social organization, ideology, and cultural changes throughout time.

These themes furnish some of the most interesting and least known documentary testimonies of the ancient **Rapanui** culture. Most of what we know comes from Georgia Lee's research.

Rock art is widely found on the island, accounting for more than 4,000 motifs. They are visible in places such as beach boulders, the finest stone pillows (**ngarua**), some isolated blocks like **Te Pu O Hiro**, with its clear-cut allusion to the **mana** to attract fish, or enormous panels (**papa**) displaying hundreds of motifs, such as those found at **Omohi**, **Hanga Ho'onu**, **Papa Tataku Poki** and, particularly, the set of carved blocks known as **Mata Ngarau** at **Orongo**.

This rock art is expressed by different techniques, such as painting, linear carving or incision, bas-relief, and in certain cases, intaglio.

Paintings with mineral pigments (**kie'a**) were concentrated at certain sites, especially at **Ana Kai Tangata** (page 50), the **Motu Nui** caves, and inside the houses of the **Orongo** Ceremonial Village. They are related to the **tangata manu** ceremony, but pigments were also painted on some of the **moai**, for example, to represent tattooing on the neck.

The best known representation is the **tangata manu** figure, generally carved in bas-relief, which is associated with the image of **Make Make**, the creator god, and the **komari** (vulva) motif, a fertility symbol.

This characterizes the second historical phase of **Rapanui** cultural development, occurring between the seventeenth and the late nineteenth centuries.

The abandonment of the megalithism of the preceding phase signified a profound change in society and in broad aspects of the culture. Nevertheless,

noteworthy evidence of continuity is the basalt **moai** known as **Hoa Haka Nana Ia**, which was placed inside a house in the **Orongo** Village.

The front of this exceptional **moai**, measuring 2.5 meters high, is classic, while the back exhibits the typical motifs of the new political and religious order: **tangata manu**, **komari**, and the **ao**, a double bladed paddle representing power.

This mix has even been observed on some of the **moai** left abandoned in the **Rano Raraku** quarry.

Although it is still not possible to date petroglyphs with any certainty, apart from those associated with the **tangata manu** phase, it can be conjectured that the oldest motifs are those carved with fine linear incisions.

The motifs are widely varied, including certain anthropomorphic figures, zoomorphic figures (predominately marine species, chickens, and lizards), a sparse representation of plants, mythological figures, and mainly geometric designs, ranging from manifest naturalism to complex abstractions.

Understanding the original meaning of these motifs and sets of designs, along with protecting and conserving these figures, presents a present-day challenge.

Sometimes, the name of a site provides information about its purpose, like in **Papa U'i Hetu'u** (observatory or marker of the stars) at **Poike**; **Moko Arangi Roa** (a legend) at **Puna Marengo**; **Te Pu Haka Nini Mako'i** (holes for making **mako'i** seeds roll, an old game which is shown on a panel as three small holes together with a large canoe and six roosters) located to the north of **Tahai**; **Papa Tataku Poki** (a legend) facing **Ahu Tongariki**; **Manini O Hera** (a legend) at **Vai Tara Kai Ua**; the spirits of **Kuha** and **Rati** at **Anakena**, etc.

Some of the most interesting motifs carved in bas-relief, besides the **tangata manu** and **Make Make** figures, are on the **Ahu Nau Nau** seawall at **Anakena**. It displays a pair of birds, an anthropomorphic being with a long tail, small fish, and a series of geometrical figures.

Alongside the remains of a large unfinished **ahu** nearby there is also a large polished basalt block (**paenga**) with a dolphin-like figure in bas-relief, which probably represents a magical fish or one that figured in some myth or legend (Georgia Lee, through personal communication).

The importance of ocean resources and their political control and magical influence are widely expressed in the petroglyphs concentrated in the old territory of **Miru**, where the royal lineage occupied a large part of the northern and western coasts.

Figures found in abundance include outrigger canoes (**vaka ama**), fishhooks (**mangai**), and extraordinary varieties of seafood, especially tuna (**kahi**) and sea turtles (**honu**). Also, sharks

*Hidden by lichen on the basalt block (**paenga**) this beautiful bas-relief shows a strange composition: a dolphin tail but in vertical position; two dorsal fins which do not exist in any known species, and a head with a swordfish-like point whose symmetric lower mandible does not belong to any kind of swordfish.*
(after a Fondart Project by J.M. Ramírez and Piru Hucke; stamping by Toni Tuki)

*Representation of an octopus (**heke**) on a panel at the **Papa Vaka** site on the La Pérouse coast across from **Ahu Ra'ai**. The harmless water makes the design stand out.*

Rock paintings are one of the most fragile kinds of documentary testimony left from the past. The pigments are slowly fading away due to the devastation of nature and vandalism. Several of the painted slabs from the interiors of **Orongo** houses were removed to be treated in an effort to preserve them. It is clear that they would be better protected for the future in the museum. The paintings at **Ana Kai Tangata** and at **Motu Nui** are at even greater risk.

Rock art was an aesthetic expression and a means of communication in use up to the end of the nineteenth century, when European ships were painted on the walls of **Orongo** houses or carved on the chest of a **moai** at **Rano Raraku** (page 75).

This is clear evidence of how awesome such vessels must have been for the islanders at a time when the only watercraft left on the island were a few canoes made of boards lashed together.

Recently, the art of rock carving has been revived as part of extensive endeavors to rescue the **Rapanui** culture. Young islanders have carved images of reality based on traditional models in a few new sites for petroglyphs on the island.

On the other hand, progressive erosion has been affecting the ancient petroglyphs, which in some cases have suffered a total loss of their motifs. Likewise, vandalism and construction work during the twentieth century, especially in the urban area of **Hanga Roa**, have meant the disappearance of entire blocks with carvings, such as at **Hanga Piko**, or the block with

(**mango**), octopuses (**heke**), and now vanished species, such as the dolphin, the seal (**pakia**), and the whale have been depicted. Highly stylized images of mythological crabs (**pikea**) also appear.

Among the more outstanding expressions of rock art, executed in bas-relief and intaglio, is a stone block called **Hoa Hoka** (page 48) found inside **Rano Kau**. Large mythological marine figures are combined with an exceptional delicacy.

Unfortunately, this masterpiece was marred by vandalism of the most despicable kind, the carving of names and dates over the ancient images.

*A turtle (**honu**) carved on a lava panel in the **Omohi** area on the northwest coast (the chalk application was not made by the authors).*

astronomical carvings that vanished during the construction of the **Mataveri** airport runway.

At present, the most serious problem is the intrusion of animals on panels with petroglyphs.

Rain, wind, temperature changes, spreading plant roots, and, in particular, the buildup of lichens are all natural phenomena that adversely affect the preservation of petroglyphs.

Man's destructive acts, both conscious and unconscious, vary widely: writing names and dates, deepening existing lines with different kinds of implements (including stones and chalk) to make them more visible, and tracing copies or making stone rubbings using improper methods.

The **Rapa Nui** National Park has undertaken a prevention program directed, first of all, at educating and spreading the word, as well as providing physical protection for certain sites by building dry stone walls and fences to keep out animals.

However, the underlying task is to establish an appropriate land distribution in order to ensure that grazing areas are available for these animals outside the park.

With the aid of Fondart (Chilean Fund for the Arts) and the participation of groups of young islanders, a project was recently carried out to rescue and protect sites with petroglyphs.

The technical problems involved, such as eliminating lichens or applying solutions to prevent remarking, need to be addressed by conservation specialists. Foreign organizations such as the World Monuments Fund are working towards this end together with Conaf and the National Park, but it is absolutely essential to encourage the community at large to participate more actively in the protection and conservation of their own cultural heritage.

The Ocean and Fishing

The sea held no secrets for the Polynesians. Many generations had used it to travel thousands of kilometers. Navigation experts acquired knowledge beyond all techniques.

The people who arrived at **Rapa Nui** must have navigated in the most seaworthy of vessels invented in the entire history of mankind: the catamaran.

Gliding over the ocean in this double hull canoe, with sails capable of withstanding the wind and equipped with a thorough knowledge of astronomy and the signs of the sea, those sailors laid out the paths of communication over the planet's most extensive body of water: the Pacific Ocean.

Over time, they adapted to different environments, developing different navigational and subsistence resources in their ocean surroundings.

On **Rapa Nui**, the only type of vessels referred to are small outrigger canoes (**vaka ama**) made with pieces of board joined together with vegetal fiber rope. These are mentioned in the accounts of the first Europeans who came in contact with the islanders in 1722.

By that time, access to sea resources had become much more limited than the restrictions imposed by the former aristocracy.

However, traditional accounts and the current knowledge of island fishermen show us an extraordinarily rich world, despite the smaller supply of marine resources as compared to other Polynesian islands and the lack of a lagoon protected by a coral reef surrounding the island.

In ancient times, the most prized fauna such as tuna (**kahi**) and turtles (**honu**) were reserved for nobility. Their capture was prohibited (by **tapu**) during most of the year. Deep sea fishing in the **vaka ama** was reserved for the wisest fishermen (**tangata rava ika ma'a**) and expert sailors (**tangata tere vaka**) and was strictly regulated by the **miru** aristocracy, which controlled the most important lands on the north and west coasts.

During the winter months, only the royal canoe (**vaka vaero**) manned by a select crew could be taken out for fishing. Anybody who ate these products was contaminated by the **tapu** and had to live in isolation for a time.

Deep sea fishing was done at sites called **hakanononga**, which were located by lining up with visible landmarks, i.e., relief features, towers

*This 8.3-centimeter-long bone fishhook, called **mangai vere vere**, composed of two human bone pieces and a bunch of hair for use as bait. The barb was joined to the grooved base of the stern and tied with **hau hau** thread or a fine human hair braid. It shows the high degree of technical refinement reached in old times.*

(**tupa**), stone mounds (**pipi horeko**), or an **ahu** while at sea. The version of the **Hotu Matu'a** legend, as revealed in the manuscript recounting the traditions of **Pua Ara Hoa,** tells how **Ariki** experts identified and named a dozen of these **hakanononga** while sailing around the island before coming ashore at **Anakena**.

Lunar phases and magic were crucial in fishing, a universal theme that takes on a special flavor in Polynesia. **Rapanui** fishing techniques and tools exhibit a close relationship to those of the Marquesas Islands.

Fishhooks can be separated into two main categories: the small **ro'u** and **piko** made of bone, used by women in coastal fishing, and the larger **mangai ivi**, fishhooks made of animal or human bone (**mangai ivi tangata**) or polished basalt (**mangai maea** or **mangai kahi**). A special kind of fishhook was the compound fishhook, made in two parts, both of which were of bone, although a few polished stone barbs are also known.

Fishing, **kahi**, seemed to hold a special importance, considering the amount of work involved in making polished basalt fishhooks. The true effectiveness of this type of hook in fishing is highly debatable.

Areas called **hakakainga** located 500 to 1,000 meters offshore were used to raise **ature**, the fish used for bait when fishing for tuna, after the **tapu** was lifted at the onset of summer.

In addition, other areas were set aside as special fishing areas (**hakaranga**), such as deep pools (**rua**),

mollusk-free rocks some 100 meters from the coast (**toka**), and the bays (**hanga**).

Techniques for fishing and harvesting marine products also included the use of a variety of nets (**kupenga**); traps (weirs made of stone walls for capturing fish at low tide); slip knots on two pieces of wood to capture eels (**here koreha**); a net at the end of a piece of wood (**hura**); the use of a net while swimming (**tutuku**); nocturnal lobster (**ura**) harvesting with the aid of torches (**puhi**); deep water diving while holding one's breath (**ruku ruku**), especially for gathering **ura** and **rape rape**, prized crustaceans; hook-and-line fishing while swimming on the surface (**hi**), among others.

As for the use of harpoons in ancient times, the only type known is a bone harpoon found at **Anakena** (page 95), similar to those used on the Marquesas Islands, with barbs, a rounded tip, and a center hole for joining it to the staff.

Harvesting the scarce mollusks and small fish found on the coast was a task for women and children. The rugged, rocky landscape made it easy to grab many by hand: small fish (**ra'emea, vare paohu, paroko, patuki**); octopuses (**heke**); small crabs (**pikea**); sea urchins (**hatuke, vana**); and some mollusks (**mama**, **takatore**, **pure**, and **pipi**).

The environmental crisis that hit prehistoric **Rapa Nui** resulted in the intensive harvesting of more accessible resources, since, with the lack of raw materials to build vessels, deep-sea fishing in more productive areas was difficult.

Today's overexploitation of species such as the lobster makes them hard to find and places them in danger of extinction. Also endangered are the small mollusks (**pure** and **pipi**), whose shells are coveted for use in handicrafts, and coral, which is heavily gathered to be sold as souvenirs.

ROCKY CLIFF AND CRYSTALLINE SEA AT MOTU NUI AND MOTU ITI

The Underwater World of Rapa Nui

Trumpet Fish (*Toto amo*)

Due to the island's extreme isolation in the middle of the Pacific Ocean, a unique underwater ecosystem developed by mixing the flora and fauna of both the rocky ocean floor and the coral reefs.

Beneath the ocean surface lies a breathtaking underwater landscape of lava-formed cliffs, caves, arches, and platforms similar to that of this island born of a volcanic explosion.

Because of the short platform around the island and the water temperature of 22º C, coral does not grow in sufficient amount so as to form reefs like those seen off the coasts of other Polynesian islands.

However, the few coral species found here are spectacularly developed, as can be observed in the "*Porites*

Page 131. (above) Lava flow forming underwater arches.

Page 131. (below) Squirrel fish (*Marau*). Live grouped in caves.

The two fish below are endemic, i.e., found at **Rapa Nui** only. Angel fish (***Kototi para***) found at depths of 10 meters or more. It is very restless and lives among the coral (left). Wrasse (***Kotea hiva***) can be found in rocky areas at 20 meters depth and greater. It is very confident and curious (right).

*Two butterfly fish (**Tipi tipi hoe**) near a sea urchin, with a coral formation in the upper portion and multicolored sponges adhered to the rock in the lower portion.*

lobata" formations. The largest of these measures around 5 meters in diameter and is located 18 meters deep in **Hanga Roa** Bay.

The water is so clear and transparent that visibility averages between 30 and 50 meters. This is due mainly to the fact that the water is poor in plankton and to the absence of rivers, ports, sewers, and industrial waste. All these factors help keep the water clean and crystalline.

Another feature that is important to stress is that the sea drops to great depths at a relatively short distance from the coast.

Due to **Rapa Nui**'s isolation, approximately 25% of the fish are endemic; they are not found anywhere else in the world. The local marine fauna includes over 150 species belonging to 65 different families.

The **Rapanui** underwater world could be summarized in the following phrase: a colossal scenery submerged in the deep blue and decorated with corals and multicolored tropical fish.

*Jacks (**Po'opo'o**).
Live grouped in caves. They have nocturnal habits.*

Tattooing, Body Painting and Mutilation

Tattooing is a widespread tradition in Polynesia and undoubtedly provided the roots for this custom in **Rapa Nui**.

Both tattooing and body painting were an aesthetic expression as well as a symbolic language.

The application of pigment dyes under the skin was done with needles (**uhi**) made of flat bird bones and teeth sharpened at one end, used to mark the incisions where the coal-black pigment obtained from a variety of plants was introduced.

Designs gathered from documentary sources of the previous century show that the process developed independently over time.

These are generally linear geometric designs applied over large areas, especially on the thighs and legs, or geometric patterns with lines and circles around the forehead. One design that was painted on a **moai** of **Rano Raraku** consists of vertical chevrons on the neck, making opposing angles starting from the center.

Other characteristic symbols are those of obsidian spear points (**mata'a**), ceremonial dance paddles (**ao**), and plants.

In recent years, as a result of a new appreciation for traditional culture, some young people have specialized in tattooing techniques, recreating **Rapanui** aesthetics of traditional tattooing, but especially using motifs from rock art.

Tattooing was clearly linked to the individual's social rank and was applied throughout one's life to mark each new status, depending on sex and social position.

On the other hand, body painting was more widespread, as described by 18th and 19th century Europeans. Covering the entire body with combinations of background colors and contrasting designs, even dyeing hair with the sacred color red, using mineral and vegetal pigments, gave greater freedom to individual creativity.

Regardless, there were standard patterns for certain occasions, such as religious ceremonies, community

*People appearing on the following pages belong to the **Rapanui** ethnic group.*

*This beautiful feathered headdress was made of (1) **mahute**, decorated with (2) shark vertebrae, (3) small shells (**pure**) and (4) **ngaoho** seeds.*

tangata manu at the moment of his anointing as religious and political leader in the succeeding stage.

Mutilation of the earlobes, very important as a body decoration, was one of the most characteristic symbols of the aristocracy. First a cut was made in the earlobe, and pieces of rolled bark were inserted so that, as they opened up, the skin would slowly stretch. As the individual grew, larger wooden disks were inserted in the lobes until adulthood was reached.

A particularly memorable and amusing European reference to this practice was the description of an islander who was not wearing his disks and had looped his earlobes over the upper rim of his ears.

Tattooing, body painting, and earlobe disks can be found since the **Ahu-Moai** phase. However, the older **moai**, in the more natural style, do not have the artificially lengthened ears.

These "short ears" (not to be confused with **the Hanau momoko-Hanau e'epe** issue), which are the oldest **moai**, should not be interpreted as part of a different migration, and even less as a different race of people. The lengthened earlobes are not a genetic feature but rather a cultural modification and could have developed independently on the island, just as the **pukao** on top of the **moai** was developed to show powerful groups.

celebrations, or family events, like mourning.

The basic pigments were black, white, and a variety of shades of ochre, from light to reddish tones. The color was mixed with animal fat or sugar cane juice to help it adhere to the skin.

Since paint was primarily applied with the fingers, it was not possible to obtain fine designs like those used in tattooing.

The best information on the use of pigments refers to dyeing the hair with red **kie'a** (as represented by the **pukao**, associated with aristocracy), and painting the shaven head of the

The Living Culture
Tapati Rapa Nui

Tapati Rapa Nui is a festival that can last up to two weeks. During this time, the island's people preserve their ancestral customs through songs, dances, and other ancient traditions in an effort to recover their origins and keep alive the culture they inherited from their ancestors.

During this event, two or more families form alliances to support their respective candidates for pageant queen. The winner is chosen based on the points obtained by her group in the different competitions (artistic, cultural, and athletic). Nowadays, the ceremonies and customs of the ancestors are followed by more modern activities. Total points earned for each competition determines who will be chosen as queen.

There is a high level of participation, not only by islanders still residing on the island, but also by those who return from all over the world to support their clan especially for this celebration.

Maintaining a cultural identity and personality to preserve their history is important to everyone.

These activities are usually held during the last week of January and the first week of February. Most tourists visit the island during this period, since this is the best opportunity to experience the **Rapanui** cultural legacy. The weather conditions are also favorable for this festival because it is the warmest and the least rainy time of the year.

This festival is also called simply **Rapa Nui** Week and was first celebrated in 1968, when airlines started their regular flights to the island, thus ending its eternal isolation. Since then, it has been held every year without interruption and has successfully fulfilled its mission of encouraging islanders to value their culture. This celebration has enabled the inhabitants to revitalize the customs, beliefs, and traditions inherited from ancient **Rapa Nui** and to share them with the world through the media and the many visitors, most of whom are tourists attracted by this unique event.

Some of the competitions not only revive the culture and make it better known, but also have stimulated interest in certain folkloric activities, such as music and dance. New music and dance groups have evolved, along with craftsmanship skills as a result of stone or wood carving competitions.

The competition of growing the largest agricultural products or catching the most fish also encourages the development of these activities in everyday life during the rest of the year.

The introduction of melodic elements and musical instruments which are foreign to the island, such as the accordion and the guitar, have given rise to new artistic expressions reflected in competitions that involve an accordion and a **Rapanui** tango, for example. Some non-artistic activities include soccer (played with a ball made of an animal bladder), boat racing, horse racing, etc.

As new competitions are introduced, others that have proven unsuccessful are eliminated, turning the competitions into a dynamic search process.

In the following pages, we will explain some of the competitions, many of which are held yearly since they have become a tradition over time and attract both competitors and the public alike.

*For many years, on the shores of **Anakena** the **Mata Nui Tu'u Hotu Iti** cultural group has recreated the arrival of the mythical King **Hotu Matu'a**, accompanied by ancient songs and dances.*

CHANTING CONTESTS

The **Tapati** generally begins with the inauguration of a handicraft exhibit in which **Rapanui** artists, both men and women, show their best work to the visitors and the community. Here we can find remarkable sculptures carved in wood or stone, and especially small replicas of the large **moai** or the mythical **moai kava kava.** Women display exquisite crafts made of **pipi** (tiny shells), garments with feathers, necklaces, head ornaments, and many others.

An exhibition of photographs and paintings is inaugurated at the same time. The paintings frequently contain subjects from past and present **Rapanui** culture, demonstrating a strong influence from Polynesian origins and traditions.

Outstanding among the different forms of ancient chants are those sung by grandfathers (**koro**) and grandmothers (**nua**), with renditions of the melancholy **riu** and **ute**, including a variety of funeral compositions (**riu tangi**), chants calling for rain, or of love or thanksgiving. The chants of praise (**ate**) or festive songs (**kai kai, ei**) are sung with no other accompaniment than the voices themselves in beautiful polyphony and the percussion of small stones.

The **Koro Haka Opo** is a singing contest among rival music groups. Each group sings five songs in a row, none of which may have been played previously by any of the competitors. After three to four hours, as many as 100 different songs may have been presented.

Gastronomical Contest
A 'atitunukai

Only women participate in this contest. This is an excellent opportunity to display their culinary skills while preparing typical **Rapanui** dishes, one of which is **ura auke**, lobsters with seaweed cooked in an oven dug in the earth (**umu**). **Moa ta'o**, a chicken dish with sweet potato and **taro**, is also cooked as a curanto in the ground.

Koreha tunu ahi is a barbecued eel.

Other more modern native dishes are also important in this contest, including **ika mata**, commonly known as "cebiche" on the continent. This consists of raw boneless fish diced with onion and various vegetables, depending on the recipe or the cook's creativity, and seasoned with lemon, salt, pepper, oil, and garlic to taste. Raw **rape rape** or lobster may be used instead of fish, or may be served along with it.

Po'e is a kind of sweet bread (similar to muffins) made of a dough of sweet potato, ripe banana, manioc, **taro**, or pumpkin, with some flour, sugar, and butter. This raw dough is wrapped in banana leaves and placed together with

A Dish of "Cebiche"

the other foods among the hot stones. When cooked, it is a kind of sweet bread relished not just by the islanders, but also those trying it for the first time find it to have a pleasant flavor. At home, **po'e** is usually prepared by pouring the dough into a metal mold and baking it at high temperature for about 30 minutes or until brown.

The most typical cooking method is the **umu**, which is common throughout Polynesia and in the south of Chile, where it is known as "curanto", a word of Mapuche origin. A wood fire is made in a 70-cm deep hole in the ground. Round stones are placed over the fire and heated until they are red hot. Then the raw food, wrapped in banana leaves, is placed on top. Red meats are placed at the bottom, closest to the hot stones, as they require longer cooking times. Then a layer of leaves is placed for insulation, on top of which are laid poultry and fish, requiring less time and lower cooking temperatures. On top, again separated by layers of insulating leaves, vegetables such as **kumara**, **taro**, corn, etc. are placed.

All of the food is covered with banana leaves and with a thick damp cloth, which is then covered with soil and left to cook for about 2 hours.

There are more than 6 varieties of curanto prepared in different fashions according to what is being celebrated. They differ from one another mainly in the ingredients being used.

In fact, at the beginning of the **Tapati**, there is an **umu tahu**. This is a propitiatory curanto. In accordance with ancient rites, a white chicken is

A dish of
Rape Rape

cooked in the ground with hot stones, and when it is opened, the food's steam is given to the spirits as a petition for good omens. The funeral curanto is called **umu takapu**.

Other typical foods are **Rapanui** stew, which is made of lamb, beef, **taro**, sweet potato, and manioc. **Maila'u** consists of grated green banana mixed with milk. **Tunu ahi** is a kind of barbecue in which stones are laid on a wood fire, and fish are placed on these hot stones to be cooked with a bit of salt for seasoning.

In ancient times, the so-called **umu pae** were used for cooking (page 54). These generally consisted of five stones (**paenga**) cut in rectangles and inserted vertically in the ground.

To make fire, a hardwood stick was rubbed over a grooved **hau hau** trunk, igniting dry grass or moss placed near the area of friction. This process took about 15 minutes and was performed by the older women, called **ruau ahi miro hika**.

The agricultural product competition seeks to promote cultivation activities, and especially aims at preserving such indigenous species as the 7 varieties of banana (**maika**), tubers (**uhi, taro, kumara,** manioc), pineapple, watermelon, etc. Year after year, farmers proudly display their success in improving their products.

LARGE AND SMALL CARVINGS COMPETITION

WOOD AND STONE

This competition is partially dedicated to carvings of the classical stone or wood **moai**, as well as specialized contests for carving such figures as the **Vai A Heva** (page 90, a human face in the rock at the **Poike** Peninsula), fishhooks (**mangai**), or obsidian projectiles (**mata'a**). Likewise, contests are held for painting on **mahute**, the fiber cloth produced from the bark of the shrub of the same name, painted with multi-colored designs inspired by **Rapanui** graphics.

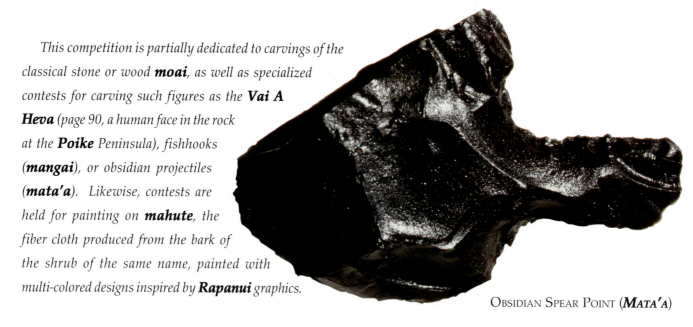

OBSIDIAN SPEAR POINT (**MATA'A**)

Rapa Nui Farandula
and Costumes Festival

*This part of the **Tapati** incorporates floats in which each group portrays or revives a legend. Of course, each float is decorated according to the chosen legend, and the more floats presented means more legends reenacted, which is highly beneficial for preserving the culture. Each float's participants belong to the same family group, which enhances the importance of the family within the society and which, in ancient times, represented the hierarchical power each tribe had within society.*

Sliding on Banana Tree Trunks

Haka Pe'i

Hurtling down the 45° slope of the **Pu'i** hill on banana tree trunks, rivals of this competition can reach speeds of up to 80 km per hour as they slide some 120 meters downhill.

In this contest, two banana tree trunks are firmly tied together and a small piece of wood is attached at one end on which the competitor places his feet. No other means of protection are used.

This game was a favorite among **Rapanui** children and youth, who used to practice it on different hills. A match of both courage and physical skill, it is preceded by ritual ceremonies. Not all who start make it to the finish line. Some may suffer violent falls due to the uneven terrain knocking the trunks off course, throwing them several meters into the air, or toppling them over, sometimes with one or more somersaults. There is always an ambulance near the finish line prepared for a possible emergency.

VIEW FROM THE TOP OF PU'I

Folklore Festival

*The folklore festival is carried out in several stages throughout the entire **Tapati** with the participation of music and dance groups, some with over 90 people. Due to the importance and number of participants involved, this is one of the highest-scoring contests for the candidates for queen. All of the presentations are accompanied by a magnificent display of costumes with feathers, banana fiber, and other materials, with songs, dances, and new choreographies highlighting **Rapa Nui**'s present and past.*

Traditional Youth Songs and Dances

*This contest is to teach children and youth **Rapanui** cultural traditions, transmitting to them all of the history, lyrics, legends, and choreography of ancestral songs and dances. They also learn how to make costumes, do body painting (**takona**), and play string games (**kai kai**). Each candidate for queen presents her group, which must perform **Rapanui** folk dances and songs. It is from here that new musicians, singers, and dancers are born.*

The Triathlon
Tau'a Rapa Nui

Since there is no rest between events, only the fittest athletes compete. In this contest it is mandatory that each participant be tattooed and dressed exactly as in the ancient fashion.

During this event, swimming with **pora**, competitors must swim a distance of 500 meters while clutching a reed float that they have made previously. Oral tradition says that in ancient times the **pora** (the float) carried food from the ceremonial village of **Orongo** to the **Motu Nui** by the **hopu manu**, who were the servants to those applying to become the **tangata manu** (birdman).

A real triathlon of indigenous sports, these games include (1) canoeing in small boats made of reeds, (2) swimming with floats also made of reeds (**pora**), and (3) a race around the lake in the **Rano Raraku** volcano crater toting a bunch of bananas on the shoulders, called **aka venga**.

Working the Mahute
Tingi tingi mahute

*This contest allows women to demonstrate their skills in making **mahute**, a cloth produced from the bark of the **mahute** tree.*

Once the bark is removed from the trunk, it is beaten with a stick on a smooth, round rock. The bark gradually stretches and thins until it becomes a kind of cloth. Small amounts of water must be applied to the bark constantly to keep it damp while it is being beaten to stretch it.

*The resulting piece of cloth is then left to dry. As it is not very large, several pieces are sewn together to make garments such as loincloths (**hami**), cloaks (**nua**), **mahute** skirts (above), etc. The cloth is then painted with colorful figures based on designs or symbols from the **Rapanui** culture.*

KAI KAI
Rapanui cat's cradle

*Although not a true system of writing, **kai kai**, still in use today, is a way to tell stories using another kind of method: reciting or singing the story (**pata'uta'u**) in a monotone chant while weaving geometric figures out of a **hau hau** string.*

A specific figure, of which around 80 remain, is associated with a particular text. Many are allegories of times long gone and have little meaning to islanders today.

*Among the most interesting texts is the well-known "**Haka Nini Te Mako'i Ngau Opata**." (spin the **mako'i** seed), which can be linked to a beautiful petroglyph on the coast north of **Hanga Roa** called "**Te Pu Haka Nini Mako'i**" (the holes for spinning the **mako'i**).*

TAKONA
Body painting

Against the island's most spectacular nighttime backdrop, the young people display the art and their knowledge of body painting

BODY PAINTING COMPETITION AT RANO RARAKU

Making Banana Fiber Garments

*The trunks of banana trees (**huri**) are cut and the leaves are removed, as the trunks consist of layers or circles similar to those of an onion. Each leaf, 25 cm wide by about 1.5 meters long, is separated into fine strips cut lengthwise and set out to dry. Once they are dry, the long fibers are used to make a waistband onto which the strips are sewn, hanging down and forming a skirt which women wear at ankle-length, and men at knee-length. This garment is then decorated with small seashells (**pure** and **pipi**) and **ngaoho** seeds. There is also a contest for making similar garments out of chicken feathers.*

Working with Reeds

*In this contest, green reeds (**nga'atu**) are cut at **Rano Raraku** volcano and taken to **Hanga Roa**, where they are left to dry. Then begins the work of softening the reeds to later make them into different weaves. One of these weaves consists of a rectangular network forming a kind of rug which was used as a sleeping mat (**moenga** and **peu'e**) in ancient times.*

Horse Races, A'ati hoi

*The first horses arrived on the island at the beginning of the 1900's and were used as beasts of burden and for transportation. Horse races were first held towards the middle of the last century, and were one of the first contests introduced in the **Tapati**. Races are now held on dirt roads. A maximum of three horses, ridden bareback, compete in each race. The winners of the approximately 800-meter distance are chosen by simple elimination.*

Sea-Related Contests

As the **Rapanui** have been in permanent contact with the sea since time immemorial, there are several contests related to it.

Coastal Fishing from the Rocks

This consists of fishing from the rocks using a bamboo rod with a string tied at the end onto which, in turn, a fishhook is tied.
A small fish named **kotea** is generally caught along with other small species, which are tasty when fried.

Regattas for Women and Men

This contest begins with the construction of racing boats which the young people and adults then row in ocean competition, proving to be descendants of great navigators.

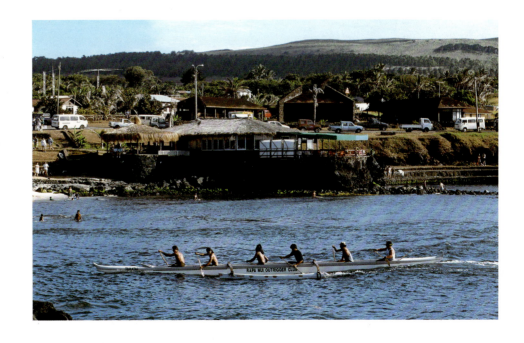

Tipitipi, a dark-colored endemic fish that lives in schools among the coral. The yellow one is a butterfly fish.

Deep Sea Fishing

The boats, with a crew of four, set out for the whole night, leaving on Saturday at 6:00 p.m. and returning Sunday morning at 8:00 a.m. With the years the amount of fish caught by each boat has been increased, in some cases reaching quantities close to 500 kg.

Submarine Fishing (A'ati Ruku)

Divers fish in submarine caves and near cliffs in apnea, that is, without oxygen tubes or other artificial breathing systems. They must catch as many fish as they can to reach the greatest weight possible. The best divers can capture over 40 kg of fish during the six-hour contest. To achieve this, they dive more than 38 meters deep, having recently made it to a record depth of 61 meters.

Eel Fishing

Other contests are eel fishing with loop traps, called **here koreha**, and scuba diving using a bamboo spear called **mata e oru**, with no snorkel, flippers, or wetsuit. In these contests the winners may catch as much as six to seven kg in two to three hours.

Collecting Small Shells (Runu Pipi)

The sea has not only been a source of food for the people of **Rapa Nui**, but has also provided some of the objects used as ornaments. In this contest, the youth display their skill in collecting shells, which will later be used to make necklaces and to decorate dancing costumes.

A Barbecue for the Entire Community (Tunu ahi mo te mahingo)

The fish caught in the above contests are then cooked on large grills. Following the customs of **Rapa Nui**'s hospitality, the entire community, including visitors and tourists, share these delicious sea products at no cost.

The Crowning of the Tapati Rapa Nui Queen

*All these festivities and celebrations end with a grand closing ceremony, generally held in **Tahai**, during which the candidate of the team that obtained the highest overall score is crowned Queen.*

Final Words

For over ten years I have waited for this new corrected and expanded version of my book **Rapa Nui** Culture. The circumstances surrounding the last few months of my seven-year stay on the island make it even more special.

Many people participated in this process. First of all, my wife, Sandra, and my children Sebastian and Valentina on the island, and Fernanda, Tomás, and Vicente on the "conti" (mainland).

Among those responsible for this experience on the island, from those unforgettable times at the Fonck Museum in Viña del Mar, I wish to affectionately mention Gonzalo Figueroa Garcia-Huidobro, the Chilean archaeologist who was part of the famous 1955-56 Norwegian expedition to the island, organized by Thor Heyerdahl. Gonzalo introduced me, thus giving me the opportunity to participate in the 1987 and 1988 expeditions, in what would be my first physical contact with the island. Above and beyond the monuments and the scientific vision, it was **Rapa Nui**'s people and magic that captivated me from the very first moment.

It would be impossible to name all the friends who should feel a part of this book. There are my former colleagues at **Anakena**, an Earthwatch volunteer group, the **Rapa Nui** Rotary Club, and especially the **Rapa Nui** National Park officials, with whom I most closely shared these seven years. Though it is unjust not to mention everyone, I feel I must recognize **Rapanui** friends like Rafael Rapu and Diana Tepano, Alfonso Rapu and Carmencita Cardinali, Juan Haoa, Nicolás Haoa and Rosita Cardinali, Hilaria Tuki, Vicky Haoa, Rafael Haoa, Juan Chávez, Petero Riroroko and Imelda Hey, Rubelinda Pakarati, Erity and Ines Teave, Bene Tuki, Emilio Araki, Juan Edmunds Rapahango, Juan Edmunds Paoa, Alejandra Valdés Riroroko, Johnny Tuki, Elvira Hucke, Piru Huke, Rogelio Paoa and Betty Haoa Rapahango, Director of the **Rapa Nui** Library, among others.

I would like to acknowledge my colleagues from the island Sonia Haoa and Sergio Rapu, and, among the visitors, I would especially like to mention Christopher Stevenson, Georgia Lee, Jo Anne Van Tilburg, Joan Seaver, Arne Skjolsvold, Grant Mc Call, William Ayres, Ruperto Vargas, William Liller, Chuck Burrows, Steve Montgomery, Nainoa Thomson, Catherine Orliac, Joan Wozniak, Antoinette Padgett, and Giuseppe Orefici.

In writing a book for a wide readership such as this, the goal was to present the technical information in a comprehensible text, without overly sacrificing the anthropological-ecological

focus in its interpretation. Interesting progress has been made over the last few years, above and beyond the emphasis on the monuments.

Most notably, recent analysis of carbonized wood remains by Catherine and Michel Orliac has proven the existence of a much more abundant and varied ancient forest and a more humid environment than previously thought. Also, Joan Wozniak's study of late agriculture provides an image of an island subject to intense agriculture, practically covered with rocks to protect the plants by mulching, as a final adaptation to the ecological disaster.

Even though some of the island's mysteries will never be solved, the knowledge of interesting, but secondary, topics, such as how the **moai** were transported or the much-discussed deciphering of the **rongo rongo** writing, could be expanded. However, the most important objective continues to be a total understanding of the culture's overall development throughout time, thus far pieced together from sketchy data and scarce ethnographic material.

There is a great deal to be done in archaeological terms, but the most urgent problem under the current circumstances is to protect the threatened archaeological patrimony. First of all, it is necessary to stabilize the **Orongo** petroglyph area and to protect and eventually recover archaeological sites on properties recently placed into private hands.

The future of the island, whose only industry is tourism based exclusively on this patrimony, depends on the management of a still-pending complex and difficult issue: a sustainable development policy.

I wish to highlight a fleeting reference made to the manuscript containing the "Traditions of **Pua Ara Hoa**," a subject hardly mentioned by some specialists. The importance of the original document, written in ancient **Rapanui**, was a finding shared with some islanders during a weekly program broadcast by the **Manukena** radio station, which subsequently motivated a massive distribution of copies. It was studious islanders themselves who extracted and shared all of the richness hidden in the text, above and beyond some anecdotal topics that we collected here. I believe this would be a valuable contribution to the recovery of the **Rapanui** culture, as part of a strong trend amongst some of the island youth in the last few years, despite all of the contradictions and problems.

Finally, I take sole responsibility for the text, while leaving the exceptional photographs and the enormous editorial work in the most capable hands of Carlos Huber, whom I sincerely thank for making this dream a reality.

JOSÉ MIGUEL RAMÍREZ

ACKNOWLEDGEMENTS

Gloria Acuña, Tiare Aguilera Hey, Arturo Alarcón, Viti Alarcón Rapu, Lilian Allen, Patricia Arellano Nahoe, José Miguel Astorga, Manuel Atan, Anita Atan, Ines Atan, Mata Iti Atan, Tamari'i Atan, Franceska Avaka, Mario Avila, Lucy Concha, Alejandra Chavez Rapu, Gianna Devoto, Eliana Durán, Alejandra Edwards, Francisco Edmunds, Renato Eguiluz, Alberto Fernandez, Marta Fuentes, Francisco Gárate, Michel García, César Gómez, Mario González, Ricardo Gutierrez, Julie Henderson, Carlos Ignacio Huber, Renato Huber, Maximiliano Huber, Te Pou Huke, Claudio Huepe, Hugo Huepe, Craig Lombardi, German Ika Pakarati, Luis Alberto Lathrop, Mario López, Francisco Luco, Sylvia Madrid, Juan Manutomatoma, Darrel Moulton Pate, George Munro, Jaime Munro, Yarhena Muñoz Rapu, Pascual Pakarati, Maria Angélica Pakomio, Rodrigo Pakomio, Caroline Pate, Pamela Quick, Hetu'u Rapu Atan, Hortensia Rapu Tuki, Hopo Rapu, Lynn Rapu, Restaurant Kona Koa, Tarita Rapu, Kahurea Riroroko, Jaime Rojas, Keisha Roloff Atan, Gustavo Romero, Rodrigo Sabarots, Carlos Sierra, Andrés Sommer, Paula Sullivan, Heather Sussman-Fort, Elizabeth Soto Manutomatoma, Danesa Teao, Ernesto Tepano, Francisco Tepano, Teresa Tepano, Baihere Tuki, Constanza Tuki, Ema Tuki, Johnny Tuki, Mattarena Tuki, Matunga Tuki, Sabrina Tuki, Toni Tuki, Javier Urarte, Carla Walker Rapu,

*The Municipality of Easter Island,
Museo de Colchagua. Fundacion Cardoen. Chile,
Museo Nacional de Historia Natural. Santiago, Chile,
Museo Sociedad Fonck. Viña del Mar. Chile,
Corporación Cultural de lo Barnechea (COBA).*

I want to thank all the institutions and persons listed who have in some way helped me make this book a reality, and I apologize to all those individuals whom I may have unintentionally left unmentioned.

PHOTOGRAPHS

All the photographs included in this book were taken by Carlos Huber, with the exception of those appearing on the pages numbered below, which were provided by:
Michel Garcia.
Pages 129, 130, 131, 132, 133, and 182.
Museo de Colchagua. Fundación Cardoen. Chile. Page 114.
Museo Nacional de Historia Natural. Chile. Pages 112 and 121.
Museo Sociedad Fonck. Chile.
Pages 54 (**stone pillows**), 73 (**polished adze**), 116, 117, and 128.
José Miguel Ramírez.
Pages 56 (**moai** eye), 72, 95 (harpoon) and 123.

I especially thank the individuals and museums named above for their kindness in providing me with the photographs mentioned.

UNDERWATER PHOTOGRAPHS

I thank Michel Garcia for his wonderful underwater photographs and for the information he provided, which was the basis for pages 130 and 132. He has lived on **Rapa Nui** for many years, and I wish to highlight the activities he has carried out during that period.

His diving center on the island, called "Orca", offers full service underwater eco-adventure excursions. While on these trips, visitors may feed the fish, leaving trails of bubbles, but the only souvenirs they may take are photographs and their memories, as it is strictly forbidden to break off or remove coral. Excursions take place mostly in the mornings, and diving locations vary, mainly depending on maritime conditions. The west coast is one of the preferred sites. Divers can go as far as 10-30 meters deep for 30-50 minutes. They are accompanied by instructors equipped with diving computers to assure that they return to the surface on time and thus avoid any need for decompression. Nocturnal diving permits the divers to observe and learn about underwater species that hide during the day.
The e-mail address is:
seemorca@entelchile.net

DRAWINGS

All drawings in this book were done by **Rapanui** artist Te Pou Huke.

GLOSSARY

AHU : Ceremonial platform
ANA : Cave
ANA KIONGA : Refuge cave
'AO : Authority, the wooden double paddle as a symbol of authority
ARIKI : "King" or paramount chief of the island, the first male born (Atariki) in every generation after Hotu Matu'a, along the Honga lineage of the Miru tribe. Also called Ariki Henua or Ariki Mau
ATUA : Deified ancestor, the old one, but not God in the general concept
AKU AKU : Spirit of the ancestor
AVANGA : Burial chamber, secondary burial at the recycled Ahu
HAMI : Loincloth, made of mahute
HANGA : Bay
HANIHANI : Red scoria
HARE MOA : Literally, "chicken house"
HARE PAENGA : Boat-shaped house (hare vaka) with foundations made of dressed basalt stones (paenga)
HEKE : Octopus
HETU'U : Star
HIVA : Mythical ancestral homeland
HONU : Turtle
HOPU MANU : Young men who represented a chief during a birdman competition
HOTU MATU'A : First Paramount Chief of the island
IKA : Fish; victim
IVI ATUA : Literally, "bone of the ancestor", priest
ITI : Small, little
KAI : In old times, to account; modern to eat
KAI KAI : String figures associated with chants (pata'uta'u)
KAINGA : Clan territory, the womb, or "mother-earth"
KAVA KAVA : Ribs
KEHO : Thin basalt slabs used in construction of Orongo houses
KIE'A : Red dye made from mineralized clay
KIO : Servant or farmer
KIO'E : Polynesian rat (Rattus concolor)
KOMARI : Vulva
KORO : Feast, old man
KUMARA : Sweet potato
MAHINA : Moon
MAEA : Rock, stone
MAHUTE : Paper mulberry tree, whose inner bark was prepared for clothing
MAKE MAKE : Creator "God"
MAKOHE : Frigate bird (Fregata minor)
MANA : Supernatural power or efficacy
MANAVAI : Stone-walled garden enclosure
MANGAI : Fishhook
MANU : Bird
MANU PIRI : Carved motif of two birds or birdmen facing one another
MANUTARA : Sooty tern (Sterna fuscata)
MATA : Eye; kin group or "tribe"
MATA'A : Obsidian, the volcanic glass; the spear point made of obsidian
MATATO'A : Military chiefs
MATU'A : Father
MAUNGA : Mountain
MIRO : Tree, wood
MIRU : Royal kin group
MOAI : Image, carving representing ancestors
MOAI ARINGA ORA : Statue with inlaid eyes: the "living face" of a particular ancestor
MOAI KAVA KAVA : Moai with ribs. Woodcarving representing an "emaciated man", a male spirit or Aku Aku
MOAI PA'A PA'A : Female woodcarving
MOAI PAKEOPA : Local name for modern woodcarvings, replicas of moai Hoa Haka Nana Ia
MOAI PIRO PIRO : Local name for a large moai at the Rano Raraku quarry, a model for modern woodcarvings with the same name
MOAI TANGATA : Male woodcarving
MOKO : Lizard
MOTU : Islet
NUA : Mother; cape or cloak made of mahute
NUI : Large, big
NGARUA : Stone pillow
PAENGA : Polished basalt stone for buildings; household social unit
PAINA : Ceremonial feast as well as the image erected as part of the ceremony
PAOA : Short war club; guardians; at present family name
PAPA : Flat lava flow
PIPI HOREKO : Stone cairns used as boundary markers
POKI MANU : Children-bird; Children prepared for the adult initiation ceremony
PORA : Reed float for swimming
PORO : Rounded beach cobbles used for pavement
PUKAO : Topknots; red scoria cylinders placed on top of some moai in ahu
RA'A : Sun
RANGI : Sky
RANO : Lagoon
RAPA : Small wooden dance paddle
REIMIRO : Carved wooden pectoral in crescent form, symbol of the Ariki
RONA : Sign; stone carving or petroglyph
RONGO RONGO : Sacred recitation
TAHETA : Stone rainwater basin
TAHONGA : Ball shaped ornament
TAKONA : Tattoo
TANGATA HONUI : Important elders, the leader of his kin group
TANGATA KEUKEU HENUA : Farmer
TANGATA MANU : Birdman or his carved representation
TANGATA MAORI ANGA AHU : Expert Ahu builder
TANGATA MAORI ANGA MOAI : Expert moai carver
TANGATA MAORI RONGO RONGO : Expert on reading and writing the tablets with sacred hieroglyphs (Kohau rongo rongo)
TANGATA TERE VAKA : Expert fishermen (vaka = canoe)
TAPA : Bark cloth made of mahute
TAPU : Sacred and prohibited
TOROMIRO : Sacred tree. Blood colored (toto) wood
TOKI : Stone adze
TUMU IVI ATUA : Shaman, man or woman with supernatural power over evil spirits
TUPA : Stone building like a tower
TUPUNA : Ancestor
U'A : A long wooden club with two opposing human faces on its apex. Symbol of rank for elite warriors (matato'a)
UMU PAE : Cooking place, underground oven delineated by stones (paenga)
URE : Penis, lineage
VAI : Water
VARUA : Tahitian word for spirit or Aku Aku
VI'E : Woman

BIBLIOGRAPHY

Ayres, William S.
1973   *The Cultural Context of Easter Island Religious Structures.* PhD Dissertation, Tulane University, New Orleans.
1981   Easter Island Fishing. **Asian Perspectives** XXII (1): 61-92.

Bahn, Paul and John R. Flenley.
    1992   **Easter Island, Earth Island**. Thames & Hudson, London.

Barthel, Thomas.
1978   *The Eighth Land. The Polynesian Discovery and Settlement of Easter Island.* The University Press of Hawaii, Honolulu.

Campbell, Ramon.
1971   *La Herencia Musical de Rapa Nui.* Ed. Andrés Bello, Santiago
1974   *La Cultura de Isla de Pascua. Mito y Realidad:* Ed. Andrés Bello, Santiago.

Castilla, Juan Carlos (Ed.)
1987   *Islas Oceánicas Chilenas: Conocimiento Científico y Necesidades de Investigación.* Ediciones Universidad Católica de Chile, Santiago.

Charola, A. Elena.
1994   **Easter Island. The Heritage and its Conservation.** World Monuments Fund, New York. 68 pages.
1990   Death of a Moai. Easter Island Statues: Their Nature, Deterioration and Conservation. **Easter Island Foundation Occasional Paper** 4: 50 pages.

Charola, A.E., R.J. Koestler and G. Lombardi (Eds.).
1994   **Lavas and Volcanic Tuffs. Proceedings of the International Meeting (Easter Island, 1990).** ICCROM, Rome.

Cristino, C., P. Vargas and R. Izaurieta.
1981   **Atlas Arqueológico de Isla de Pascua.** Universidad de Chile, Santiago.

Cristino, C., P. Vargas, R. Izaurieta and R. Budd (Eds.).
1988   **First International Congress: Easter Island and East Polynesia (Easter Island, 1984)**. Universidad de Chile, Santiago.

Dillon, Bryan (Ed.).
1986   **Journal of the New World Archaeology**. Vol VII, Number 1: 72 pages. UCLA, Los Angeles.

Di Salvo, Louis H., John E. Randall and Alfredo Cea.
1988   Ecological Reconnaissance of the Easter Island sublittoral marine environment. **National Geographic Research** 4: 451-473.

Drake, Alan
1992   **Easter Island: The Ceremonial Center of Orongo**. The Easter Island Foundation and Cloud Mountain Press. 97 pages.

Englert, P. Sebastián.
1977   **La Tierra de Hotu Matu'a. Historia y Etnología de la Isla de Pascua. Gramática y Diccionario del Antiguo Idioma de la Isla.** 6ª. Edición Editorial Universitaria, Universidad de Chile, Santiago (1948, Imprenta San Francisco, Padre Las Casas).

Finney, Ben.
1992   Viajando Hacia el Pasado de Polinesia. **Clava** 5: 9-39. Museo Sociedad Fonck, Viña del Mar, Chile.
1993   Voyaging and Isolation in Rapa Nui Prehistory. **Rapa Nui Journal** 7 (1): 1-6.
1994   Polynesian-South America Round Trip Canoe Voyages. **Rapa Nui Journal** 8 (2): 33-35

Fischer, Steven R. (Ed.).
1993   **Easter Island Studies** . Contribution to the History of Rapa Nui in Memory of William T. Mulloy. Oxbow Monograph 32. The Short Run Press, UK. 247 pp.

Flenley, John R.
1993   The Palaeoecology of Easter Island, and Its Ecological Disaster. In: S.R.Fischer (Ed.) **Easter Island Studies**: 27-45

Gill, George W. and Douglas W. Owsley
1993   Human Osteology of Rapanui.In: S.R.Fischer (Ed.) **Easter Island Studies**: 56-62

Heyerdahl, Thor.
1958   **Aku Aku. The Secret of Easter Island.** Allen & Unwin, London.
1975   **The Art of Easter Island.** Allen & Unwin, London.

Heyerdahl, Thor and Edwin N. Ferdon (Eds.).
1961   **Reports of the Norwegian Archaeological Expedition to Easter Island and the East Pacific.** Vol. 1: Archaeology of Easter Island. Monograph of the School of American Research and the Museum of New Mexico 24 (1). Allen & Unwin, London.

Lee, Georgia
1992   **The Rock Art of Easter Island: Symbols of Power, Prayers to the Gods.** Monumenta Archaeologica 17. The Institute of Archaeology, Los Angeles.

Lee. Georgia. (Ed.).
    Rapa Nui Journal. Easter Island Foundation. California, USA. Published quarterly since 1986.

Proceedings of the Third International Conference on Easter Island Research: Rapa Nui Rendez-vous (Laramie, August 1993). Two papers were published in Rapa Nui Journal: 9 (3), 1995; 10 (2) 1996; and all the rest (29 articles) in Vol 10 (4) 1996; and Vol 11 (1-2-3) 1997.

Liller, William
1993   **The Ancient Observatories of Rapa Nui. The Archaeoastronomy of Easter Island.** Easter Island Foundation Cloud Mountain Press. 61 pages.

McCall, Grant.
1981   **Rapa Nui: Tradition and Survival on Easter Island.** The University Press of Hawaii, Honolulu.
1993   Little Ice Age: Some Speculations for Rapa Nui. **Rapa Nui Journal** 7 (4): 65-70.

Mètraux, Alfred
1940   **Ethnology of Easter Island.** B.P. Bishop Museum, Bulletin 160. Bishop Museum Press, Honolulu.

McCoy, Patrick C.
1976   Easter Island Settlement Patterns in the Late Prehistoric and Protohistoric Periods. **International Fund for Monuments Bulletin 5**. New York.

1979   Easter Island. In: J.D.Jennings (Ed) **The Prehistory of Polynesia**. Harvard University Press, Harvard & London. Pages 135-166.

Mulloy, William T.
1961   The Ceremonial Center of Vinapu. In: **Heyerdahl & Ferdon Eds.** (pages 93-181)
1967   Easter Island. **Natural History** 76 (10): 74-81
1975   Investigation and Restoration of the Ceremonial Center of Orongo. **International Fund for Monuments Bulletin 4**. New York.
1976   A Preliminary Culture-Historical Research Model for Easter Island. In: Echeverria, G. and P. Arana (Eds.). **Las Islas Oceánicas de Chile** Vol 1: 105-151. Inst. de Estudios Internacionales, Univ. de Chile, Stgo.

Mulloy, W.T. and Gonzalo Figueroa.
1978   The Akivi-Vai Teka Complex and its Relationships to Easter Island Architectural Prehistory. **Asian and Pacific Archaeology Series 8**. University of Hawaii Press, Honolulu.

Orliac, Catherine and Michel Orliac.
2000   The woody vegetation of Easter Island between the early 14th to the mid-17th centuries AD in Easter Island archaeology. In: C.Stevenson and W.S.Ayres (Eds.). **Research on Early Rapa Nui Culture**. Easter Island Foundation, California.

Ramírez, José Miguel
1986   **Catálogo de la Colección Pascuense**. Museo Sociedad Fonck, Viña del Mar.
1988   Rapa Nui: un Milagro en el Pacífico Sur. In: **Los Primeros Americanos y sus Descendientes**. Ed. Antártica, Santiago, Chile.
1989   **Cultura Rapanui**. Serie del Patrimonio Cultural Chileno. Colección Culturas Aborígenes. Ministerio de Educación. Santiago de Chile.
1990   The Anthropological Background of Easter Island. An Outline. **Rapa Nui Journal** 3 (2): 1-2.
1991   Rapa Nui: Auge y Caída de una Cultura Megalítica. In: A.E. Charola (Ed.). **Lavas y Tobas Volcánicas**: 17-24.
1992   Transpacific Contacts: The Mapuche Connection. **Rapa Nui Journal** 4 (4): 53-55.
1993   Rapa Nui: del Arte Tradicional a la Artesanía Moderna. In: **Catálogo de Artesanía Chilena**. Universidad Católica de Chile, Santiago.
1992   Contactos Transpacíficos: Un Acercamiento al Problema de los Supuestos Rasgos Polinésicos en la Cultura Mapuche. **Clava** 5: 41-73. Museo Sociedad Fonck, Viña del Mar, Chile.
1994   Possibile Contatto con le Coste del Sudamerica (Cile Centrale). In: G. Ligabue and G. Orefici (Eds.) **Rapa Nui. Gli Ultimi Argonauti**. Erizzo Editrice, Venice. Pages 239-248.
1994   Rapa Nui: Rise and Fall of a Megalithic Culture. In: A.E. Charola et al (Eds.) **Lavas and Volcanic Tuffs**: 239-251.
1998   Patrimonio Cultural y Comunidad en Rapa Nui. In: X. Navarro (Ed.). **Patrimonio Arqueológico Indígena en Chile. Reflexiones y Propuestas de Gestión**. Instituto de Estudios Indígenas, Universidad de la Frontera. Unesco. Pages 125-131.
2000   Rapa Nui Land Management: A Personal Chronicle. Rapa Nui Journal. 14(2): 47-48

Ramírez. José Miguel (Ed.).
1988   **Clava 4**. Museo Sociedad Fonck, Viña del Mar, Chile.

Rauch, Marcos and María Elena Noël (Eds.)
1998   **Parque Nacional Rapa Nui. Manual de Capacitación sobre el Patrimonio Cultural y Natural de Rapa Nui**. World Monuments Fund and Conaf. Litografía Valente, Santiago.

Routledge, Katherine.
1919   **The Mystery of Easter Island**. Hazell, Watson & Viney, London.

Seaver Kurze, Joan.
1997   **Ingrained Images. Wood Carvings from Easter Island**. Easter Island Foundation and Cloud Mountain Press.

Skjolsvold, Arne
1994   Archaeological Investigations at Anakena, Easter Island. **The Kon Tiki Museum Occasional Papers** Vol. 3, 216 pages. Oslo.

Steadman, D., P. Vargas and C. Cristino
1994   Stratigraphy, Chronology and Cultural Context of an Early Faunal Assemblage from Easter Island. **Asian Perspectives** 33 (1): 79-95

Stevenson, Christopher M.
1984   **Corporate Descent Group Structure in Easter Island Prehistory**. PhD Dissertation. The Pennsylvania State University
1986   The Socio-Political Structure of the Southern Coastal Area of Easter Island AD 1300-1864. In: P.V.Kirch (Ed). **Island Societies**. Cambridge University Press. Pages 69-77.

Stevenson, C. M., G. Lee, F.J. Morin (Eds.).
1998   **Easter Island in Pacific Context: South Seas Symposium. Proceedings of the Fourth International Conference on Easter Island and East Polynesia**. (Albuquerque, August 1997). Easter Island Foundation, California.

Stevenson, C.M. and W. S. Ayres (Eds.).
2000   **Easter Island Archaeology: Essays on Early Rapa Nui Culture**. Los Osos and Bearsville Presses, California.

Van Tilburg, Jo Anne.
1986   **Power and Symbol: The Stylistic Analysis of Easter Island Monolithic Sculpture**. PhD Dissertation, Univ. of California at Los Angeles.
1992   **HMS Topaze on Easter Island. Hoa Hakananai'a and Five Other Museum Sculptures in Archaeological Context**. British Museum Occasional Paper 73.

Van Tilburg, Jo Anne and Georgia Lee.
1987   Symbolic Stratigraphy: Rock Art and the Monolithic Statues of Easter Island. **World Archaeology** 19: 133-149.

Vargas, Patricia (Ed.).
1999   **Segundo Congreso Internacional de Arqueología de Isla de Pascua y Polinesia Oriental (Isla de Pascua, 1996)**. Anales de la Universidad de Chile.

Vergara, Víctor.
1939   **La Isla de Pascua. Dominación y Dominio**. Publicaciones de la Academia Chilena de la Historia. Universidad de Chile.

Wozniak, Joan.
1999   Prehistoric Horticultural Practices on Easter Island: Lithic Mulched Gardens and Field Systems. **Rapa Nui Journal** 13 (4): 95-99.